Catching Butterflies

A Memoir

Catching Butterflies

A Memoir

by

Freida Barnes

LOVE
CHILD
BOOKS

A Division of Consuming Fire Incorporated
WWW.CONSUMINGFIREINC.COM

HAMPTON, VIRGINIA

Published by Love Child Books, a subsidiary of
Consuming Fire Incorporated.

A Love Child Books Memoir

Love Child Books
206 W Taylor Ave, Hampton, VA 23663

Love Child Books is a subsidiary of Consuming Fire Incorporated
Visit our website at www.consumingfireinc.com

Printed in the United States of America

First Love Child Books Printing: February 2011
ISBN: 978-1460915868

Cover design by Stephen Blackmon.

— *Foreword* —

*T*his book is a story about a bad girl who became good. Freida, the criminal, became a devoted mother, a prosperous worker, a devout believer, a good citizen, and a helper of those who, like her, have walked a wayward path. It is a dramatic narrative about personal initiative and saving grace.

C.S. Lewis paraphrased the Bible in one of his novels stating, "If God were just, who could stand it."

Freida is living proof that God's justice is tempered with mercy and love for the righteous. Despite her misdeeds, she lived with courage and integrity. And she could not have arrived where she has come today without a core of honesty and a commitment to what is truly good.

Freida is one of the few individuals I have known who actually got what she deserved, and who deserved what she got. She sinned, was punished, struggled, and obtained redemption and prosperity, both spiritual and material. She lived intensely every act of her drama. She courageously has looked reality in the eye and did not deny it.

Much or little can be made of Freida's tale. The cynic can dismiss it as just an exception to the rule that criminals never change, the naïve can take it as a blissful tale of transformation and the realist can claim she just got lucky that things went her way. As an eyewitness to this drama, I can vouch that it was all these things and a great deal more. Freida is and has been fully human in living the adventure presented here. She was not out to prove anything, or to be something she wasn't. Her efforts were halting and timid at times, heroic and belligerent as needed. Underneath it all, she was determined to be a good person and have a good life. She wasn't selfishly ambitious, but she knew that it was important for her to do well.

It was my good fortune to be nearby while this transformation took shape over the course of twenty-plus years. Despite her gratitude to the Way Back House, we did not change Freida. Those of us involved did however, support, encourage, affirm and witness her growth and development. She did not need us to walk this path, but she invited us to be a part of it. We are grateful to still be involved.

There is no meaningful dialogue in America today concerning criminal justice. There's just a lot of noise, hysteria and presumptions (and a great deal of stupidity). Politicians want to get tough, evangelists want to save the heathen, citizens want to be safe (with a minimum of expense), and it's all based on the assumption that criminals are less human than "we" are; and that they deserve whatever they get. Freida's story will prove them right—and wrong. The important lesson here is that offenders are human, and as such, they are capable of making their way, and of losing it, just like anyone else.

Yet there is an overwhelming presumption that justice is the answer, and the rougher the better. Justice is never "the" answer, nor is religion, education, rehabilitation, punishment, or the death penalty. Our complex society seems desperate for simplistic, monolithic solutions. We should neither be harsh nor weak in response to criminals. We must be open to their humanity, and welcome their capacity to change. Few stories will end like Freida's, but if we want to facilitate more outcomes like hers, sentences will need to be brought back down to survivable levels and parole and probation supervision will need to be flexible and conducive to growth and success. My forty-two years of professional work in juvenile and criminal justice agencies have convinced me that our policies and practices ignore the fundamental tenet of physicians to "first, do no harm." If we simply tried to limit the excesses of justice policies and practices, we would likely have many more stories like Freida's to tell.

Albert Richard
Executive Director of The Way Back House, Inc.

— *Dedication* —

*T*his book is first and foremost dedicated to my Lord and Savior who's grace and mercy are never failing. I would like to thank the precious gifts that God has entrusted to me... my four beautiful daughters, all my grandchildren and my great grand daughter.

Keira, Melinda, Vidella and Kiera - each of you are so very special. I love you and thank you.

I would like to acknowledge Rev. Dr. James and Rose Taylor, Keira's adoptive parents. You guys are my angels. You did a fine job. I thank you.

I thank Bishop Steven W. Banks for being the loving husband to my daughter, and father to my grandchildren that you are.

To Arlene, my big sister, as crazy as we are, I still love you. And I offer a special dedication to my brothers. To Clinton - your spirit has always been with me. And to William Jr. - keep your head up.

To Ms. Pam Slaton - thank you for helping to reunite Keira and me after so many years. I thank you.

This book is the direct result of someone giving a damn about another human being.

I've made a few mistakes in my day (more like a baker's dozen). But when I arrived at the Way Back House there were two gentlemen, Mr. Everett George and Mr. Al Richard, that did not look down on me for the crimes I'd committed, the color of my skin, nor my sex. Their only concern was for me to turn my life around. They, and the Way Back House, offered me a "second chance." With some suspicion and caution on my part, I accepted what the Way Back House had to offer.

So in retrospect, as I was writing about my misadventures, I realized that not only was God keeping an eye on me, He was placing His assigned people on my path for the moments that I would choose whether or not to accept the help offered.

There are many individuals associated with the Way Back House that contributed to my second chance. I hope they will forgive me for not being able to name them all, and still accept my gratitude. Please know that I may not be all that I could be, but thanks in part to you, I'm a lot better than I was.

I would also like to dedicate this book to all the past and current board members that support and fight for the residents of the Way Back House.

I would like to thank all the past and current staff, even those that I may have had a few choice words with. (You should know that coming from prison to any halfway house, I wasn't exactly going to be Miss Sunshine.)

I offer a special dedication for Mr. Everett George, Mr. Al Richard, Mr. Dan Matise and Mr. Tom Densmore. You may not have known it then (Heck! I didn't even know it), but you and your organization had a positive profound effect on my life. I thank you.

I would like to acknowledge Stephen Blackmon. Thank you for all your creative work and expert advice.

To Ross and Kiera Dean - thank you for answering my never ending stream of questions. You were always polite and diplomatic.

To all of my co-workers at R&J Studios - thank you for all your support and encouragement during my ups and downs with this project. You all are great.

— Contents —

Part III: Catching Butterflies

Catching Butterflies

On Children

And a woman who held a babe against her bosom said,
Speak to us of children.
And he said:
Your children are not your children.
They are the sons and daughter's of life's longing for itself.
They come through you but not from you,
And though they are with you
Yet they belong not to you.

You may give them your love but not your thoughts,
For they have their own thoughts.
You may house their bodies but not their souls,
For their souls dwell in the house of tomorrow,
Which you cannot visit, not even in your dreams.
You may strive to be like them,
But seek not to make them like you.
For life goes not backward nor tarries with yesterday.

You are the bows from which your children
As living arrows are sent forth.
The archer sees the mark upon the path
Of the infinite, and He bends you with His might
That His arrows may go swift and far.
Let your bending in the Archer's hand
Be for gladness;
For even as He loves the arrow that flies,
So He loves also the bow that is stable.

- Kahlil Gibran

THE PHONE CALL

March 5th, 2008

"Hello?"

"Hello, is this Frei–?" Static and the rustling bags and mail in my hands were louder than anything else the woman said. I'd just gotten in from work and a short trip to the grocery store.

"What?" I responded. "I can't quite hear you. Could you hold on a minute?" I set the bags and mail down, and pulled the phone to my ear again. "Ok. Sorry about that. Now, who is this? And who are you looking for?"

"Well, my name is Keira Banks. I'm trying to find a woman named Freida Barnes."

Her name was similar to my youngest daughter Kiera's name, but the pronunciation was different. "And this is in reference to what?" I thought it was a bill collector trying to get information.

There was a short pause. "Uh, this is a confidential matter for Freida Barnes. My name is Keira Banks. I'm looking for my birth mother. I was born at Booth Memorial Hospital in Queens, New York on July the 27th, 1965…"

I dropped the phone.

I couldn't believe what I was hearing.

When you've dreamed about someone for more than forty years, searched for her, and then actually find yourself talking to her over the phone, you don't really know how to react. You don't know what to say. I had imagined this day for such a long time. I'd imagined how I would find my daughter; how we'd be reunited and she would meet her sisters.

I'd imagined her running into my arms a million times, like she was five years old, me swinging her around, both of us laughing and truly happy. But I'd also imagined her not wanting to meet me, being angry about the adoption, or worse, looking down on me as a mother, or looking down on me for the life I've led.

How would this turn out? Would she want to know me? She found me, which was a good sign. But if she got to know me, would she still be happy she found me? Could she accept me? Could she forgive me? Would she understand?

I picked the phone back up.

"I'm sorry," I said. "Dropped the phone. You said you were born at Booth, on July the 27th?"

"Yes."

"Well, then yes. My name is Freida Barnes. I had a daughter that day at Booth, and yes, she was taken from me and put up for adoption. I named her Kiera just before they took her."

There was another pause. My daughter continued. "I spoke with a lady named Pamela Slaton at an agency in Manhattan. She found you through a…" She went on to tell me how she tracked me down, that she lived in Virginia with her husband and my two new (to me) grandchildren. I so wanted to hear every detail of her life, but my own questions continued to distract me. Before we got off the phone, we arranged to talk again soon.

Now, I don't like secrets. I've raised three girls – Dorothy, who we call Melinda or Hymie, Vidella, which we call Beva, and my youngest is named Kiera. I named her that after the daughter I reluctantly had to give-up for adoption. But we call my youngest Kiki. My girls mean the world to me. We've been through a lot. I pretty much tell my girls everything. I figure it's better for me to tell 'em, before someone else misinforms them. They've always known about their sister, just as they've always known about my life. We hoped together to be reunited with her.

But how would I share the story, the true story, the whole story, with this grown daughter I was meeting for only the second time? What would I tell her kids?

So many times, so many questions, so many years I was in turmoil, just mad at the world. At one point I had no desire to even live. I'd gotten so used to things being taken away from me, to never being able to depend on anyone. Boyfriends faded. Marriages failed. Parents didn't care.

I committed to writing a book. I even committed to the harder part, which is actually reliving the scenes of my life clearly enough to be able to write them down. As I replay the different things that happened in my past I've found it hard to accept that God makes no mistakes.

PART I
Chasing Butterflies

1

SERGEANT BARNES & CHINESE TAKEOUT

Blood gushed out of my nose as I ran down the stairs towards the bathroom. I cupped my hands over my face in an effort to keep the blood from staining the carpet or the walls, else there'd be more hell to pay. I could feel my left eye swelling. It was becoming difficult to see. I could hear the muffled sounds of fist against flesh coming from our room. My older brother and older sister were still in there. I don't know how I managed to get out. I grabbed the post of the stairwell using it as leverage to quickly swing round towards the downstairs bathroom. I saw Daddy sitting at the table, a huge sparerib hanging out of his mouth, a plate filled with shrimp and scallions sitting before his large belly.

He was eating Chinese takeout.

He was eating.

My sister, brother and I were getting the shit beat out of us and he was at the kitchen table, eating as if nothing even remotely violent were going on upstairs, eating as if it weren't his own children's screams coming from behind the closed door, eating as if everything were normal.

I walked into the bathroom, closed the door behind me and sat on the toilet pressing wads of toilet tissue against my nose and cried. I must have been 10 or 11 years old.

That was in 1961, but my story begins on January 9, 1950. I was born in Jamaica Hospital in Queens, New York.

Mother wasn't involved in the naming process as she tells it.

"The nurse named you, I had nothing to do with it."

And that, as they say, was that. My birth certificate has the name of my parents, the doctor and "female Barnes." Eventually my name became Freida LuRenee Barnes. And this is the story of my life, as I remember it.

*   *   *

Mother was tough. She was a stern, no nonsense woman. I don't recall any tender moments; at least she never had any of those moments with me. I don't have any cute anecdotes or mother-daughter insights that I could have passed on to my girls. Those I do recall don't really sound cute:

"Whatever don't kill you makes you stronger."

"You make your bed, you lie in it."

That's all I seem to remember.

Life started out with only three of us: Kirby, the eldest son, Arlene, the eldest daughter, and me, the stuttering, dark-skinned daughter with nappy hair. It was made clear early, I was not my parents' favorite.

"You so ugly. Why can't you be more like your sister, Arlene"? That was Daddy.

"If you stutter one more time, I'm going to slap the tongue out of your mouth". That was Mother.

"Sergeant Barnes" was my nickname for Mother. Of course, she never knew, but she was so damn hard and mean that she would have made a great hostile force against any enemy. I imagine her service in the military would have been legendary.

"Breaker, breaker 1-9. We've got an unidentified object approaching from the south south east. Over."

The radio would crackle and horrid, hair-raising screams of men would be heard.

"Save...your...selves." And then silence.

There wasn't much to my daydream, just Mother on a rampage, beating ass as usual. Instead, we ended up being her target.

Most of the beatings she'd grab the broom and start beating all of us. If the broom broke, she'd continue the job with anything in sight. Mother laid into all of us, the girls included. We were punched, kicked, thrown against walls and punched some more.

Daddy wasn't to be found during any of this. Not once did he ever intervene, come in to calm down the situation and make Mother behave as an adult instead of a wild animal. Not once.

It was the same with Mother. If Daddy commenced to beating our asses, she turned a blind eye as well. Daddy would tie the boys up with a rope or one of Mother's stockings. After the boys got some age and weight on them, they would try to get away. So daddy would actually take them down to the basement and tie them up. I never could understand how mother would allow that to go on. But there she'd be, sitting in the living room watching Perry Mason drinking Pepsi with the soundtrack of our screams playing in the background. I realized early that my parents didn't give two shits about us. And we the kids, well...we never had a chance.

Sometimes the beatings happened because the house wasn't cleaned to Mother's specifications: diapers were to be washed and hung outside on the line to dry, big bags of wrinkled clothes needed to be ironed, folded and neatly tucked into the *correct* drawers. Dishes were to be washed, dried and placed in the cupboards, floors needed to be swept and mopped and windows and mirrors needed to be wiped down and cleaned with newspaper and vinegar. Once the scent of Pine Sol filled the air we'd neared the end of our cleaning chores, but rarely did we clean the house to Sgt. Barnes specifications and beatings ensued. Most other times, the beatings just happened spontaneously. No forewarning, no cause; just the effect of a warped view of parental supervision.

When Daddy was the problem, we got it.

When work was the problem, we got it.

When the car needed to be fixed, we got it.

When the bills needed to be paid, we got it.

When the Pepsi ran out, we got it.

*   *   *

My brother, sister and I started out close, looking out for one another and keeping each other out of trouble. I thought myself the mediator, but sometimes I was so scared that I'd just stutter and nothing saved us, least of all my broken mouth. Mother really hated the fact that I stuttered.

Being the third sibling out of nine put me in a pretty bad spot from my vantage point. Not the one old enough to be in charge. Not the one to be cool with the first in line. Just the one to be the pain in the butt to the older ones.

Kirby was the oldest. Then came Arlene and me. But Kirby didn't live with us for most of my childhood. He was beat so bad one day when he was 13 that once he recovered he ran away and joined the military. He actually rode his bicycle off into the sunset, and didn't return until he was a grown man. He joined the Army. Back then a boy could lie about his age and join a military gang. Marines, Navy, Air Force. Kirby chose the Army. So it was me and Arlene. But after a while, my younger brother Clinton was born, and then I had an ally.

Clinton was cool even back then. But I had to watch him. The girls loved him. Then came Kevin, Gayle, William Jr., Maxine, and Kimberly. There was so many of us…even with the older sibling leaving the household at an early age, there was always chaos. Soon I felt like the old lady in the shoe. My childhood was changing diapers (not Pampers), fixing bottles and cleaning the house. OH! And I'd better not throw out the stinking diaper. They had to be washed, mostly by hand, then hung-up outside to dry.

Well, as time went on we got older and crazier, pretty much fending for ourselves. Mother and Daddy did keep a roof over our heads and they did drive decent vehicles, but it was all for show.

Daddy, at one time, owned two or three rent houses. That was out of the ordinary for a black family at that time, especially a family of eleven. So as I was saying, we had to look out for one another.

We had plenty of gang fights in Jamaica. Kirby and Arlene went to P.S. 140. The other high-school that was full of bad-ass kids was P.S. 141. On any given weekend, after any basketball game or even at the roller-skating rink,

**Daddy and
the Barnes Kids (left to right):
Back - William Jr., Daddy, Gayle, Kirby, Kevin. Front- Maxine & Clinton
(Kim is in front of Clinton)**

there was sure to be a fight. And you could count on that
fight spilling over to Monday at the 3:30 bell. Almost all
of the fights took place on Merrick Blvd. And you had to
walk past our house to get there. So by the time kids passed
by us, the fights were at full steam. We lived in a big corner
house right down the street. Almost every day there would
be a fight. On the weekends, we would watch the winos
fight. Then Daddy would come home and have us chase
them away from our property.

The few times we would sneak out the house or be
allowed to go over to the other side of town, we'd find

ourselves in "Hollis Queens." It seemed there was this group (gang) there, called themselves the Green Leafs. The thing was, if you didn't have a leaf (off a tree) these kids would commence to kicking your ass. Most of the fighting and stuff was just that " kid stuff." At times there were more serious fights; kids getting cut, some getting broken arms (my brother Clinton did most of the breaking) and of course back then they had the zip-guns. So that was pretty much the fun stuff we had in our neighborhood. Knowing how to fight and when to run fast helped us survive.

Most of the time Mother and Daddy would work at night so they could get some rest while we were at school. Then we'd come home with the chores to be done.

"Drill Sergeant Barnes", I would mumble. Making a joke of her craziness just always seemed to lighten my pain. I learned a lot about how to fight from her. I learned how to weave and bob. I learned how to take a punch. I learned how not to cry or show pain. So for that I'm not complaining. She really was right. It did make me stronger.

Looking Back

My thoughts are that as the saying goes, "Hurt people, hurt people." Dysfunctional families are not uncommon. The degree of the dysfunction is the question. When I was about seven or eight years old I said to myself, "If I ever have children I would never treat them this way." Sometimes all a child needs is a hug, emotional support and to be heard. I believe that a child should be both seen and heard; not dismissed and certainly not abused.

Somehow I instinctively knew that our home was not a healthy, normal household. But how does the next generation break the cycle of anger, rage, and bitterness? I believe that forgiveness is a beginning. We must forgive others and forgive ourselves.

2

THE HUSTLER FROM NEW ORLEANS

We moved to a new area of Queens – St. Albany's, which was a lot like the other side of Queens, just a bit of a step-up from Merrick Blvd. At the time, my best friend's name was Theresa Pitts. She was probably my favorite person in the world, though I can't say I knew very much about friendship back then. Theresa was always one of those prim and proper girls. On top of that, she was cute, so the other girls hated her. So whenever it looked like things were about to get rough – like she might get in a fight at school, I took up for her. I wasn't a bully, but I just hated to see anyone get picked on. Well I was also sorta crazy, with brothers that would fight anyone. So I could pretty much come to school looking wild out, and sometimes I did. I might have a cool outfit one day and a black eye the next, but no one said a damn thing. (Back then the teachers didn't give a damn about the troubled kids, not that I would tell them anything anyway.) But Theresa was my friend. She was definitely the only one I could really talk to. And together, between the beatings, we had our adventures.

I don't think I'll ever forget the day Theresa and I got to tap dance at Count Basie's house. That was a big deal. He used to have summer pool parties for some civic group or something. Now, how I got to be picked to be in the show at his house is still a mystery to me. I think it was Theresa's mother that arranged everything, but I never found out for sure. The fact of the matter is I was always told that I dance like a white girl. I don't really know what we looked like in there doing our extra excited version of prim and proper Jazz tap. But I know they didn't ask me back the next year. Needless to say, that was the end of my dancing career. But I did get to see some of Count Basie's house. It was the best damn house ever!

We had to see the area by the pool to know how to practice our routine. I also got to talk to his wife and daughter. The daughter was in a wheel chair and didn't really seem to know that Theresa and I were even there. I felt so sorry for her. She had such a great house to live in. She had such great parents. I don't think I ever truly understood what her condition was. I just felt sad that she had to be in the wheelchair.

But the impression left in my head of a nice house with a pool was a good thing. Sometimes just seeing another picture, seeing other possibilities, can plant a seed.

Now we also knew that James Brown had a home in that same neighborhood. Theresa and I used to hang around the area, hoping to get a peek at him. We never did get to see James Brown. But we sure had fun waiting for him.

*   *   *

Now and then Daddy took us back down to Merrick Blvd. Merrick had some of the greatest shops, at least in that day. Daddy would stop and buy sweet potato pies from this mom n' pop store. You could buy either these little single size pies, about three inches across, or a full size pie. The guy that made the pies would have them lined up in the window and as people passed by, you just had to stop and buy one. The look and smell of those pies... hmmm! To this day, I still remember how good they were. Those were good times in Jamaica. Such a small thing... I remember a three-inch pie. Daddy didn't make sweet potato pies at home, but he did eat those with us.

There was a barbershop close by where the boys would sometimes get their hair cut. It didn't happen often, as Daddy hated spending money. Daddy just complained so much about spending a dollar it was embarrassing. He would get all loud in the shop, or store, "Why this cost so much? I'm not paying if I have to wait. I got $2. Take it or leave it". He was a character!

An old-fashion drugstore with a soda fountain sat on the corner. They had the best egg-cream soda and ice-cream cones. I loved going there for desert. But we rarely did. Mostly we would go there to buy mother cigarettes (Pall Mall Red). The look of those packs is also burned into my mind.

Daddy was working for the Jewish bakery, so we were filled up with free Jewish goodies. Oh! Mother she could do a sweet potato pie. She had her special moments when I'm sure things at our house were normal. And I'm not condemning her for anything good or bad. She was just like any other black woman with a large family back in the day… except that she would kick our asses.

*   *   *

My immediate family started out in Harlem. Mother and Daddy both worked at the famous Hotel Theresa on 7th Avenue. It was a big deal back then. Fidel Castro stayed there… at least once. Malcolm X was there all the time. Or so Daddy said. That's where he and Mother met. Mother was born somewhere in Virginia, whereas Daddy comes out of New Orleans. Somehow they both landed in Harlem.

They must have been quite a couple. Mother is dark skinned, like dark brown sugar, with long thick black hair. Daddy was the opposite, passing as white any time he wanted. They must have stirred up a lot of problems for themselves. You know back then people were color struck. Funny, it's easy to talk as if that's not still true today. I'm sure that couples that seem mixed today still get looks, have family and "friends" make bad jokes. But you could still get hurt back then, hurt real bad. Sadly, it was just as bad in the black community as it was with white folks. In that day, Harlem was one of the best places in America for black people to be. Still, if you got light skin, pretty features and long hair, the haters were out to get you. Some were jealous. Some were bitter. Others thought you were better than the rest of us. So mixed couples lost each way.

I don't really know what brought Daddy to New York. I heard tales at one point that he'd been run out of New Orleans, but I never could get the true story. But I guess that's why we don't know anything about his family.

We don't know much about mother's either. We kids only knew that Mother's mother, Grandma Jesse, died in a car crash when I was still young. That, and that she and I had the same birthday. I recall

The Hotel Theresa

seeing her maybe three times, but those visits weren't long, and those memories are hazy. She and Mother didn't get along. We did get to meet Aunt Claire. She lived in a cool apartment one 135th St. Aunt Claire was like a bohemian-hippy back then. Her pad was where the musicians hung out. You can only imagine the drugs and stuff that went on back then. But she passed on. It's not like we as a family were close to her. I saw her maybe three times in my life, as I remember. And she was only a short train ride away. My sister Arlene kinda grew up to be Aunt Claire. She still lives

My parents.
I always thought my mother was pretty. It
would be a long time before I understood why she didn't seem to think so.

42

in New York. I'm not sure, but maybe Kirby or Arlene got to know a little bit more about her and Grandma Jesse. But as for my father's family, none of us knew. We never heard from anyone, and he never said anything.

One of the main things I remember about the house Mother and Daddy kept, was that appearances were everything. I remember one Christmas, we had lights and all this shit outside but inside we had nothing. My brothers and sisters and I were so scared. In our house you'd better not even mention Christmas, no less a present. Once or twice we joked (far from our parents' ears) that they were starting some new religion. If they were, it sure would have helped if Mother or Daddy had at least told us. We didn't know what to think. And we really could have used a good laugh.

Daddy's way of being funny was usually putting on these horrible creature masks and scaring the hell out of us. He was really kinda childish with a mean cruel edge.

One thing I can say, is that in his way Daddy was fair. He hated everybody equally. You were either too black, too ugly (his favorite), too fat, or too stupid. Everybody else had a problem except him. I often wondered what kind of childhood he had. What made him so suspicious of people? How did he and Mother feel during the holidays when most families shared their lives with relatives? I'm trying to remember old photos of aunts, uncles, cousins… Nope. The only photo that comes to mind is a faded picture of

Grandma Jesse. As a child you just don't realize how things like this affect a person.

I believe Mother was probably a lot stricter with us than she might have been, because she had so many kids. She was also hard on us to hide a lot of stuff that went on with her and Daddy. I'm sure some of their stuff happens within most families. Some could have been handled better. But I suspect mother stayed on overload, was always on the verge of losin' her mind, so her personal defense was her coldness. Much of her disappointment and anger at other things was unevenly taken out on us.

Some of Mother's arguments with Arlene were just the normal stuff. I thought they were normal. But in retrospect there was far more going on than I realized.

My mother hated herself because she was dark skinned. I'm as sure of that today as I am that the Earth is round. Mother was raised during the era when black people were given the position of either house nigger or field nigger... and that was determined by how dark or how light your skin happened to be. Mother was considered a field nigger. And I don't think she ever let that go. I believe that's why she took so much shit from her husband. She married a half-white man, and must have thought it would cover up her blackness. Her strength came from the inner depths of her hate. Mother's hatred of herself always seemed to boil over to Arlene. I can still hear Mother shouting at her.

"You little yellow bitch!" Other statements could also

be heard through the halls.

"Oh! You thank you one of them pretty bitches?!" Then came the beatings and the pulling of the hair. I used to be so scared of my mother, and I felt so sorry for my sister. She would be bloody before Mother was through. Me, I would find a quiet hole and pray to God she wouldn't come after me too.

But most of these particular beatings came right after something else, like the leather coat incident, or that look that pretty Ms. Wilson gave Daddy as she walked by the house. Yeah, Mr. Barnes had more shams and girlfriends throughout our childhood years than I can count. It's a mystery why mother didn't kill his ass. Instead, she just beat the shit out of us. As long as she was able to put that red ass lipstick and thick-as-pancake make-up on (that left a two tone line on the side of her face), she kept going. She went off and faced her bosses and co-workers, speaking very proper with lies jumpin' out her mouth each time it opened.

When things went wrong for Mr. Barnes, the whole house felt it. Things like insurance companies not paying a claim. These were usually scams, like when daddy took the television down to his friend's house and told the police we had a break-in. We didn't know what to do when he set fire to the place. It was a little fire. He'd planned it all. He even knew exactly where it would stop.

But when those insurance companies did pay, oh!

There was joy in the house. He would even go out and by pizza or Chinese food and we'd all be eating and laughing. Now and then he would even play a little bit of blues and do his slow drag dance in the front room. He'd say, "Come on Frances and dance!" Of course she would refuse, saying some proper dumb shit like, "Oh William, I've got to get some sleep for work tomorrow". Then we would have to clean up the messy ass kitchen and daddy would disappear from the house. By the next evening you could hear Mother and Daddy fighting. I never knew the true story or what that kind of behavior meant 'til years later. To this day I don't know how many outside kids Daddy has. But it was a lot. No wonder Mother was pissed all the time.

Looking Back

When I was a child I didn't understand all the challenging dynamics my mother faced. Now I see that she is a product of her times – when dark skinned women had a difficult path to walk. In addition to a house full of kids to feed, mother had to deal with a husband who was a larger-than-life, colorful character who was rumored to have had plenty of girlfriends.

Once when mother and I were on better terms, I asked her why she stayed with my dad. I was never given a real answer but I do understand the need for a woman to weigh her options. The question is... did she really have any options? Where could she go with nine children? How could a black woman in the 1960's, with minimal skills and education, relocate and start over without the support of a husband? Today women have greater options available and far more organizational and spiritual support is available to assist women in transition.

60 DIVISION STREET

*M*oving from Queens to Long Island was considered a big deal; "movin' on up" as *The Jeffersons* later put it. Yes. When we got to the New Castle area of Westbury, New York, as they say, we had arrived! My father purchased a big house on a corner lot. 60 Division St. It was a nice place – at least far nicer than anywhere else we'd lived. The day we moved was the first time I ever saw live pigs; I mean wide-open farmland up close. It wasn't even that far of a drive, but life seemed different there. New Castle definitely was not inner-city New York. However, not all change is good. Three days after we got there was also the first time I was ever called a nigger.

It was a pretty normal day. I don't remember anything else unusual about it. There was just some stupid white boy in the junior high school. I guess I, being skinny and new, looked like an easy target. The kid just underestimated the nutcase he was dealing with. I was never one for being picked on. I may not have been able to fight Sgt Barnes, but anybody else who came at me the wrong way was fair game. This poor boy just didn't know that. *And*, he didn't know about my brother Clinton.

Clinton was special, and he and I were close. Clinton could sing and dance just like James Brown. He was very good in math. I struggled with the numbers in school, but he just would say to me "it's easy Freida, just do this or that and that's how you get to the answer." We learned a lot together, like how to get the house cleaned up at lighting speed and how to cut the grass and straighten out the garage before mother and daddy got home. I think we both really learned how to fight from Mother. Mother would beat our asses. And we took notes. That stupid white boy thought that he and his three friends were going up against one scared and skinny little black girl. He had no idea what was coming.

Back in those days there was a strong Italian influence in that area. The mayor was Buffilino. There were other Italian families, the Sappolinos, or something like that, which everybody knew. Then there was the family that owned a huge junkyard. They dealt in a lot of stolen goods, and illegal activities for years. I would later find out that a lot of these families had quite a reputation. There were Italians all over the place. My point is, Westbury was owned and run by tough influential and very powerful Italian families.

I had no idea what was really going on behind the scenes. I didn't care. But I sure wish someone in my family had seen the handwriting on the wall when we arrived there. Would it have made a difference? I don't know. Knowing myself at the time, probably not. I still would have beat that boy's ass like I did. Clinton still would have jumped in when his boys jumped in. We looked out for each other. We were close like that. But if someone had told us, at least we would have had a better idea of what to do afterwards.

At that time Westbury was just starting to deal with the integration of blacks coming from the inner city. It was also dealing with the migration of blacks from the southern states. During that same period immigrants from Cuba, Haiti, Jamaica, folks from all over, started moving to

Integration was starting and a lot of folks weren't happy about it.
The New York City Nine had recently met with the Mayor.
Photo Credit: New York World - Telegram/Library of Congress

Westbury. The crime rate skyrocketed. It was just madness. During all of this, here we were trying to fit in as some of the earliest new black kids at a white school. Things just went from bad to worse.

I never really liked any of the time I spent at that place. I had a few kids I called friends, but not many. I thought I was tough, and I acted like it. But in my defense I will say, it wasn't a nice and warm place to be. If you weren't tough, you certainly learned quick enough, or the other kids ran over you.

I felt like I was running all the time. Looking back, I think I was running from myself. But whatever I was running from soon ran me right into trouble. I got the worst of most deals, not being old enough or wise enough to fully understand the implications of what I or we were doing. So I got the neighborhood label as a loose wild child. Don't get me wrong. I'm not saying I was innocent. I'd done my share. I would pretty much take up any dare someone could think of. Some of those fights I started. I also learned that if you can back it up then it ain't bragging. I couldn't stand people that bragged and I couldn't stand a bully. I found myself in a lot of situations where I was on the line for taking up someone else's cause. So I did have to learn to be a little more selective in the company I kept. (Friends I have learned are highly over-rated.)

That particular day, I was at lunch. I forget the boy's name. Tony, or Bobby, or Vincent or something. I didn't care. I was minding my business. I was on my way to class when he started his jokes. The first couple didn't really bother me. They irritated, but I didn't have time. But when he started calling me the "N" word…he crossed the line.

More than what he said, I remember that day because of how glad I was that I hit him. The feeling I had beating his ass was wonderful. I could feel the joy of punching him in the gut. Clinton had my back when his friends tried to step in and assist him. They were surprised when Clinton started to handle them. Not one, not two, but three other guys were actually ready to help this boy whip my ass. So beating him felt good all down to my toes. It made me feel better. Later on, it even made it easier to take Sgt. Barnes' crap at home.

I don't know if that boy ever did live down how badly the skinny black girl beat his ass. But I do know that it didn't make things easier for us. We got into some other scrapes because of it with the regular neighborhood kids, (black and white). You know how it is when you're the new kid in town… As we tried to assimilate into our new schools and neighborhood, things just went from bad to worse.

*   *   *

Although Clinton and I had each other, and managed to give each other a little reprieve from the hell we had at home, some of my other brothers and sisters were not so lucky. Kirby was already gone. Arlene was soon to follow. However Arlene did not join the Army. She landed in the mean cold streets of Harlem. She went right back to the life mother and daddy had moved us away from…the inner city. I'm sure that somewhere… deep down, my parents were trying to save us from the lifestyle of the streets…but something just went wrong.

Knowing well how much Mother hated her, it didn't come as a surprise. As pretty as Arlene was, she could have gone into show business or something. She was the full package. She could have been the next Lena Horne. Arlene could have passed for white back during her youthful years. Yet as beautiful as she was, she got no encouragement from Mother. I don't think Mother ever let go of the light skin / dark skin issue. If you were light-skinned you were automatically pretty, no matter if you had big buckteeth or googley eyes. If you were dark-skinned you were automatically ugly, didn't matter if you had high cheekbones, Chinese eyes and Indian long black hair. If you were dark–skinned, "you was ugly." Mother was truly beautiful, but she was dark-skinned. And I believe with the passing of time and her own disappointments, Mother developed a black heart, or maybe she had a dark heart that just got blacker…

Mother must have felt like Arlene was her biggest competition when it came to Daddy's affection. I can't say Mother was wrong about that. After all, Daddy would always brag on how pretty his daughter "Arlene" was. He'd actually wanted to name her "Orleans" after his birthplace. He always spoke well of New Orleans. There was never any mention of his mother except to say that she was white and she didn't raise him. He would reminisce about Mardi Gras, and say "the prettiest women in the world are from New Orleans." I do remember him going to Mardi Gras a few times, but that was as much as Daddy would tell us about his childhood. I've never even seen one old brown photo or learned anything else about his life as a child or young man growing up.

We did know that Daddy had some dealings with a more famous Mr. Barnes there in the city. The rumors were that Nicky Barnes was Daddy's nephew. We weren't allowed to talk about that in the open. But the man did kind of look out for us a number of times out there in New York. I guess there must've been something to it, though I probably couldn't prove it if I tried.

Arlene was supposed to go with Nicky to Africa to see the "Rumble in

the Jungle". I understand that a lot of folks still call that the biggest fight in history. Nicky's entourage was big and memorable, and they went in force. I remember how excited Arlene was about the trip. She didn't go though. Turned out there was some problem with her passport. At least, that's the story I got. All I really know is that that was a hell of a time. I guess thats why I couldn't get my self together to watch the movie "Americian Gangster". Living that shit is nothing like a two hour movie. Death is real. Ruined families, broken dreams; some families never recover. Some of the sounds and smells still affect me to this day.

We kept company with a lot of infamous characters. Just like the song "Street life" says, you'd better not get old.

The Rumble in the Jungle. Ali and Foreman.
I've always wondered how Ali would've done against Sergeant Barnes.

Mother's indifference didn't bother Arlene one way or another. Arlene was a free spirit and didn't need or want Mother's encouragement or approval for anything. And unlike our older brother Kirby, Arlene would talk back, argue and curse Mother out like she was some woman on the street, which was the other reason why Mother whipped her ass so much.

As I remember it, Arlene and I often went to school in raggedy clothes with cuts and bruises from the previous night's beatings. Sometimes, Mother would dress Arlene and I in matching outfits. One such outfit came from Mrs. O'Rourke.

Mother once worked for a white woman named Mrs. O'Rourke. She used to go on and on about how beautiful Mrs. O'Rourke's home was, how the silverware was always nicely polished, the kitchen always clean and sparkling, the floors always freshly vacuumed and the bathrooms pristine with floral scents. She especially loved the window treatments, the beautiful drapery and nice fabrics Mrs. O'Rourke used. It was Mother who did all the work to keep the house looking as good as it did, yet she never mentioned that. No, she only talked about how great Mrs. O'Rourke's home was and how shitty her own house looked with us good-for-nothing kids not appreciating anything. Because Mother worked for Mrs. O'Rourke doing all of her cleaning, that meant my brothers and sisters and I were left to clean the 'shit-house Barnes household', and it was never quite good enough.

Mother also talked about how lovely Mrs. O'Rourke's daughters were, and how they were proper and well-mannered children. "Why can't you be more like the white children?" she'd often yell as she beat us.

Mrs. O'Rourke had given Mother two dresses for us. They were brown with really big collars. They must have looked cute and befitting on Mrs. O'Rourke's girls but they did absolutely nothing for Arlene and I. The color was wrong for our skin-tone and the dresses looked pretty dumb on us. Still, Mother insisted we wear them.

"Keep them nice and clean or it's your asses," she'd said sternly. Mother was always proper when she talked. To this day she still speaks with an air of superiority, yet always with a tone of menace and hatred or just pure evil.

Arlene and I hated the dresses. They just looked big and dopey on us. While walking down the street the big collars would flap in the wind and other kids at school started calling Arlene and I 'the Dumbos,' because of the way the collars flapped. It looked like big elephant ears. Kids used to laugh at us when we wore those dresses and at first, it didn't bother us too much. Or maybe Mother's threats just replayed in our heads and we thought it was in our best interest to just ignore the taunts. But, one day it just became too much and with Arlene's deteriorating relationship with Mother, she no longer cared. So she fought.

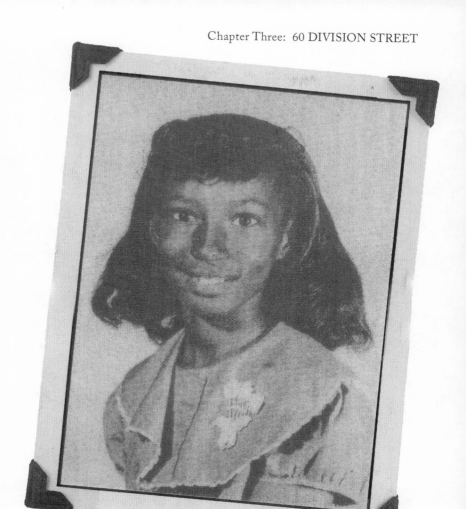

Lord knows I hated that ugly-ass dress.

We both fought that day, but I made damn sure not to get that ugly, hand-me-down dress torn or messed up in any way. I knew when I went home it was better that I would be beat up and bleeding, than to have torn that dress. It better not even have a wrinkle in it.

Arlene's dress, on the other hand, was torn at

59

the collar.

Sure enough, when we got home Mother was in a rage. Arlene got beat up for the dress being torn. I got beat up just for being there. I never had to iron but one dress after that, because Arlene ended up throwing hers away. Unfortunately, I had to wear mine quite a few more times before I was allowed to let it go. I even had to wear it for class photos at the end of the year. Most of my childhood photos were lost throughout the years. I guess it was never really important to Mother to keep up with them. But somehow an individual photo of me in that dress at the age of nine is still around. Arlene must have kept it.

I don't have many photos of my younger years. It just seems a shame the only photo of me is in that homely dress with the big collar.

*   *   *

But it was the coat that finally pushed Arlene out; that gorgeous damned leather coat. Well, Mother, the job and the coat.

Daddy brought home a badass leather coat one day from the second-hand store for the women of the house. The gangster-like coat was unbelievably cool. It was real leather with all the trimmings, satin black with two-inch buttons and a belt that tied at the waist. It was a three-quarter, the softest sheepskin leather and just oozed class.

As I said, Daddy thought Arlene was pretty. So, since he'd only brought the one coat, and he wanted to see Arlene in it, he told my mother and Arlene to share it. Mother worked at a plastic toy factory on Jamaica Avenue. She worked nights while Daddy worked during the day. Mother would wear the leather coat to work in the evenings while Arlene and I would take turns wearing it to school. Arlene was in middle school and I was still in grade school. I must have looked like a damn fool wearing that big ass coat to school the few times I got to wear it. But it was leather! I would have paid money to wear it if I'd had any.

Well one Saturday... Mother and Arlene had an argument over the coat. Arlene wanted to go some place, and Mother wouldn't let her wear it. I didn't get to hear all of that argument. But right after that, Arlene stopped going to school. Arlene was not the one to go anywhere looking tacky. She would steal clothes out of stores just so she could look good going to school. At one point Mother would mock her saying she was tryin' to be the neighborhood glamour girl. Arlene could have been a model.

Steal you say? Yes. We never had any restrictions placed on us when it came to getting money. If we were able to get away with it mother and daddy didn't care...as long as it was to benefit them as well. I remember Arlene just not being able to deal with mother, and it spilled over into her ability to do well in school, so she just stopped trying to get along with mother.

Looking Back

Upward mobility can be a blessing and a curse. Although we moved into a better neighborhood, we still had the same issues. We were inner city kids attempting to integrate into white suburban life. Our family never dealt with the internal, fragmented dynamics of our family...we focused on the externals... the house, the car and keeping up appearances.

What happens when a family begins to fall apart before your eyes? How do you begin to put the pieces together to solving the problem of broken hearts and broken relationships? First and foremost I had to face my own issues and begin the healing process for myself. It all began to change when I made the decision to become better than my past, more forgiving and more understanding.

4

SUNDAY DINNER

"Whatever don't kill you, makes you stronger!"

I've heard Mother's expressions echoing in my mind my entire life. I've come to learn the truth in her words. I've also come to learn that some stuff that doesn't kill you surely can screw you up for a long time. Sometimes forever.

I met Wellington Cobb one Thursday evening after school. He was a good-looking boy. And he was nice for the most part. I wasn't used to nice. We dated briefly, the way teenagers do. And for the time it lasted, I liked it. I sure liked the way he talked to me and treated me. Actually, I liked it a little too much. Before you know it, I was pregnant. I was 14.

As you might guess, telling my parents did not go well. And it didn't help that my mother was already pregnant with my little brother Kimberly. During the first few weeks of my pregnancy I had no idea my mother was also pregnant. Whenever Mother was pregnant, she was actually more irritable. It was even easier to get her fussin', cussin' and whoopin' ass.

I guess by that point, I didn't expect help. My parents had clearly shown how they felt about me in general and when I'd only made little mistakes. During the 60's it was considered the biggest sin of all for a young, unmarried daughter to become pregnant. "WHAT WOULD THE NEIGHBORS THINK??? Hell, even the wealthy white girls were sent away from their community so they would not embarrass their families. So the arguments did not surprise me. Being called every curse word I'd ever heard before. The beatings and tongue lashings did not surprise me. *You made your bed. You lie in it,"* and such. But finally, the arguments and fighting just got to be too much for me. I began to feel sick. To this day I think it was more from the fighting than any morning sickness or pregnancy complications.

I left home on a Friday afternoon. Well, I left school and just didn't go home. I imagined what that day's yelling would be, and I just started walking. I walked for miles. It wasn't in circles, but it wasn't in a straight line either. It's not like I had anywhere to go. My little boy friend wouldn't even talk to me let alone try to help. The rumors had already spread in the neighborhood. I was damaged goods; the town tramp. I just couldn't, wouldn't go home.

In retrospect, I'm glad I left. I don't think I would have survived in that house. I'm sure I would have ended up as a cold case.

I spent some days on the streets. But I quickly learned that living on the streets is hard. You never really sleep. At least not people new to the streets like me. And definitely not young girls all by themselves. You never feel safe. You never feel comfortable. You never feel clean. And it's different than being by yourself. You really feel alone. That part didn't bother me as much as it probably bothers some. There weren't all that many people in my life that I really felt good around before I ran away. So I definitely didn't miss them. Except Clinton. I did miss Clinton.

For safety's sake, I finally decided to go to a shelter. I needed some real sleep, I needed some real food, and it was getting cold. Someone directed me to a dark, gothic building on Eighth. I walked there and knocked on the door. I told them I was tired and had no place to go, and they took me in. I became a ward of the state. Soon after, I heard that they were required to tell my parents where I was. But as neither Mother nor Daddy ever came to see about me, I assume that nothing at home had changed. The shelter was still the best place for me to be.

The Nassau County Children's Shelter was, let's say, a growth experience. I hadn't known what to expect before I got there. But what I got was definitely educational. Years later I learned that during that winter of '64 and spring of

'65 Mother told people I'd gone away to some art school. Well, we didn't do much art, but you could say it cured me of my last thoughts of childhood. But in retrospect, I never had much of a childhood, so maybe I can't say that. God knows it wasn't a normal or happy one.

One of my younger brothers…William once told me that his oldest memory of me is running through a field chasing butterflies. He says I used to do that all the time. I was obsessed with them. It seems odd to me that I have no recollection of that… none at all.

*   *   *

At the shelter that's about all I had: shelter. For anyone going into a situation like that during the 60's it was pure hell. Back then there weren't many regulations and little to no community accountability as to what went on inside those hellholes. Some of the people who worked at those shelters were more sadistic than Mother. I had to fight for everything.

The only difference I felt between the shelter and my own home was that I had the ability to fight back. These women weren't my mother. They weren't blood relatives and I was free to dish out as much pain as I was expected to sit back and take. Some of those women were big and tough. Most of them were middle-aged Italians who had a distaste for black people in general, let alone a homeless black child.

I'd been at the shelter for about six months. By this time all the matrons knew I was pregnant. I wasn't one of the favored children for obvious reasons, therefore I got slighted on just about everything. I was often given the worst work detail, less time to shower and one of the best tricks up their sleeves was giving me less food during the dinner service.

Sunday supper was the best meal of the week, supposedly. Maybe meatloaf with mashed potatoes and a roll, or spaghetti and meatballs with garlic bread, or fried chicken with mashed potatoes and peas. A decent meal with all the trimmings, you know.

Well, this particular Sunday I wasn't in the mood for any of the head matron's shit. I was pregnant, hungry and definitely fed up with the matron's bullshit tactics. She was a big, fat and mean-ass Italian lady. As I said, she didn't really care for me, nor I her, so I avoided her as much as possible.

As the meat portion of the meal was given out we were all seated at a high, round table. There were about six of these tables filled with women and snot-nosed little kids, plus other teens around my age. Now I admit, I was almost eight months pregnant at the time, and constantly uncomfortable, so it didn't take much for those fellow homeless children to become loud and obnoxious snot-nosed little brats in my eyes. But that particular matron had acted ugly with me from the moment I arrived.

The matron dished out the food, going from one child to the next. Eight of us were seated at my table waiting for our portion. She went from child to child to child. She dished it out and put the serving tray back on the rolling cart in the middle of the dining hall. She nonchalantly strolled back to her place at the head table, bent her head and began to say grace.

No one was allowed to eat until she reached her seat and finished saying grace. But I took a look at my piece of chicken and I was pissed. As usual, I got the short end of the stick, or rather, the crappy piece of chicken; the piece that falls off from the larger portion of the chicken wing. So basically me and another girl got a bony chicken nugget.

Everyone's head was bent, grace is nearly over and I'm so mad I can't see straight. I can't even halfway listen to this bitch because I'm pissed off about this little ass chicken nugget sitting on my plate when I'm hungry as hell. So, I jump up, scramble over to the head table and snatch the biggest piece of chicken off the matron's plate. I started eating it right then and there, right in front of her wicked face. All I could hear was one loud, synchronized gasp from all the other kids and matrons because by now I'm up on her table, face to face with the woman, eating her piece of chicken.

Some of the other kids started eating like pigs, just shoveling food into their mouths. Others started yelling and screaming.

"This whole fucking place is unfair!"

"Yeah, this place stinks!"

Food started flying across the dining hall. Fried thighs and drumsticks hit people in the face. Mashed potatoes slopped against the wall and slid down. People slipped and slid trying to walk over the peas. It looked like a scene out of *the Little Rascals*. And during all of this, that evil-ass matron just stood there, backed up against the wall… scared as hell.

The male matrons from the boys' side of the shelter came in and carried me out. But the grin didn't leave my face for a long time. That was the best piece o' chicken I ever ate.

Soon after that I was transferred out of the shelter.

Sunday Dinner helped shape my defiance of authority. Likewise the shelter and its head matron were shaping my ass for my future misadventures in prison.

Looking Back

At fourteen I was a child in an adult situation. I was initially homeless. How is it that the shelter becomes a better choice than going home? Home for me was not an option. I feared that my parents would literally beat me to death. I had good reason to fear my parents. I had seen the brutality towards my siblings first hand. I had witnessed the disappearance of my oldest brother and their indifference to it. I had witnessed the harsh treatment of my sister Arlene and her desperate need to run away. I knew that my offense was a death sentence. To be pregnant at fourteen in my parent's house was the ultimate blow to my family's carefully crafted image.

Is it asking too much for parents to show compassion and understanding when a child makes bad decisions? Is it asking too much for parents to remember what it was like to be a teenager and to be confused and lacking judgment? I only wanted my mother's help and unconditional love.

5

GOODBYES

I was shipped to an adoption home in Queens that was close to Booth Memorial Hospital. That was by far the most caring and peaceful place I'd ever lived up to that point of my life. There was a mix of young girls and young women there; some black, but mostly white, middle to upper class. Most of us actually got along. I guess we could understand each other's stories. There were at least three other girls who'd run away... though we never talked about that around the staff. A number of the girls' families had turned on them. Tricia's parents had actually told her to change her name. But most of the girls still had some place to go once they left the house... as long as they were traveling alone.

There was a foreign woman that worked there named Miss Leena. I think that's how it's spelled. She was very helpful. I think she was from Viet Nam, but I never asked. I don't remember that much about her clearly, but I do remember that she helped me name my baby. We had a long list of boys' names. (I was sure I would have a boy. I was told by one of the matrons as I left the shelter, "all that fighting you be doin', you gonna have a boy"). We had a few girls' names too, just in case, but I was *sure* I was gonna have a boy.

One girl's name that stood out to me was Kiera. I was so taken by that one I asked Miss Leena to help me find out what it meant. They didn't have computers back then. And though I was an avid reader, all I could come up with were names close to the spelling, like Kayla or Kara. But I could not find Kiera. Miss Leena did finally find something suggesting the name was Native American. It had a spiritual meaning, but I didn't fully hear her or completely understand it when she told me what it meant. Well, whatever it meant, I thought the name Kiera just had a special sound to it.

I recall reading the book *Treblinka* while I was there. It described the horrors of the Jewish Holocaust in one of the German concentration camps. I remember wondering if I was that Jewish girl, caught up in her situation, would I be able to get through it all? But some of the names in that book had a nice ring to them. (When you're nine months pregnant everything is about your baby.) I especially liked the name Rivka. Another girl at the house had given me the book. That was also her name. She was one of the other young girls living out the last months of her pregnancy there. But how would a little black girl wear a Jewish name? Something about it, and connecting her with that story, didn't seem quite right. So as my time came to give birth, the decision was made. And on July 27th, 1965, Kiera Barnes was born. I was 15.

I don't remember much about the childbirth. I'm pretty sure I was doped up. My older sister Arlene says she was there, but I don't remember her presence. I do remember, however, being able to hold my child. I remember how beautiful she was. I remember the length of her smooth silky hair. I remember that her features looked Native American. It made me confident I'd picked the right name. I remember how soft her cheeks were. I remember the sound of her breathing. What her breath felt like on my hands, on my shoulder. I remember the face of the nurse that took my daughter from me. There was some pity there. She clearly hated this part of her job, though that didn't help me at all.

I remember letting my daughter go. I remember the way my chest ached as she was taken from my hands; a physical throbbing pain that would stay with me for years to come. And I remember crying afterwards. I remember feeling even more alone than when I was living on the street.

That was easily the worst day of my life, and I've had

some bad days. If nothing else, the past eight months had taught me that I was in no position to take care of her; to feed her, to keep her safe and secure; to treat her the way she should be treated. I couldn't even take care o' me. And there was nothing I could do about it, but cry.

That's the day I started praying. *"Lord Jesus, watch over my baby. Lord Jesus, keep her safe. Lord Jesus, let me meet her again, someday."* I cried and prayed, ached and asked, would it ever be ok?

*   *   *

The following few days were a blur. Not fast. Just all mushed together.

Once I was discharged from the hospital, I was shipped to a girls' home and reform school in Valley Stream, Long Island. The housemothers were a group of nuns. They were a bunch of haggard old women. Most of the other girls were white, aged from 13 to 21 years. If no one in your family came for you, you stayed there until you became of age, which I think was either 18 or 21; something like that.

To say I have many memories of that place, fond or not, would be a lie. By that point I'd really started to block some things out. I didn't want to remember it. I didn't want to remember most of my childhood. I didn't want to remember Sgt Barnes, but I knew I'd never quite be able to shake her. The thing I did want to remember was Kiera. I was determined and committed to see her again. I vowed to find her. Once I was in a position to be good for her, I would find her. The rest I let blur.

This home was not like the house for pregnant girls. I do know that I was not liked. I didn't have one friend in the place. I tried running away a few times, but I was always brought back. It was quite clear my parents didn't want me back. So that's where I remained until, by some people's standards, I was almost an adult.

I was released, or rather expelled from the reform school just before I turned 18. They wanted me gone and told my mother I didn't fit in. By order of the courts I was to be released to her. I vaguely recall my older brother, Kirby having something to do with it. I could be wrong. Like I said, some things in life are just so painful that we choose to blur the details.

So I was taken back to the house in Westbury. But even more than I thought had changed by the time I got home.

PART II
Running in the Fields

FREEDOM

*D*ivision St. seemed a weird place to return to, and even stranger to call home. I was back with my family, but I couldn't sleep any better there than I did on the streets.

Many things had changed during my years away at "art school", as my parents called it. I don't recall any visits. No one even sent a letter to let me know what was going on, or how my younger brothers and sisters were doing. I guess the irritating mail from the children's courts was all the correspondence mother felt she had to deal with.

Aside from the fact that there was an addition to the family [my youngest brother Kimberly had been born on July 7TH, 1965… two weeks before my first child] I found that Clinton was gone.

Apparently, those early fights from our high school experience had escalated.

The enemies he'd made in that first fight with the racist boy never let it drop. Clinton had a number of run-ins with the guys from that family. And it culminated in a fight with the mayor's son. Sadly the boy brought a knife to the fight. During the scrap, Clinton took it from him. They got the boy to the hospital in time, thank God. Clinton did a few years. I'm not sure of how much time he actually got. I do know he went away up state for a long time, and I do know he did over a year in solitary lock-up for that.

But fighting followed Clinton. It did his whole life. Race battles followed him. He developed a reputation, which stuck with him. He took up martial arts, and people said he was pretty good. That was easy for me

My unforgettable brother Clinton.

to believe. I'd seen Clinton fight before he had any formal martial arts training, and I remembered our first master fighter. We all had to deal with Mother's genuine "black belt."

Black Panthers, Bobby Seale and Huey Newton. Clinton loved their militant stance.

Actually, I found that Clinton had done a lot while I'd been away. A couple of his friends told me that he took up with the Black Panthers for a while. For those who don't know, they were a radical group of strong black people who stood up to police brutality back in the 60s and 70s. Yeah, some were crazy. But those were crazy times. And some of us were just sick of gettin' beat. It would be a while before the Panthers knew what to do with women... if they ever did. But I could definitely relate to their resistance to oppression.

Clinton's friends told me that he met Malcolm X. He was friends with one of Malcolm's bodyguards.

They also told me he started sellin' reefer.

I guess it was just the quickest way to get cash. When

he did get out he was on his own. He sure wasn't coming back to Division Street. And I didn't blame him. It just wasn't home anymore.

My relationship with my parents was strained beyond repair. Daddy couldn't, or I should say wouldn't even look at me. And Mother… It didn't take long to see that this wasn't going to work. It would never work. That would never again be my home.

I couldn't stay with my parents. And even though I worked and imagined going to college, my mind became fixed on the new goal and love of my life…Freedom.

* * *

I went back to high school and stayed in long enough to meet James Outlaw – a "bad boy" from a family that my parents detested. I started hanging out with him because he was just cool. He had a jazzy sports car, dressed nice and always seemed to have money.

Yes, his name was Outlaw. James T. Outlaw. You'd think a last name like that would have told me to think twice. But actually, at the time, his house was a great place to be – the best place I had to be, anyway. He was the new adventure that took my mind away from my problems. His family seemed to like me and didn't mind me hanging out at their house.

The Outlaws owned a dry cleaners in town that did pretty well. At least, money never really seemed to be an issue. They were a pretty fun bunch; nice people over all compared to my family. At least, that's how I saw it.

His mother was very much the head of the family even though his father worked very hard. They had nine kids, and didn't seem to mind other kids, other people in general being around. I think that after James got to know me and my brothers, he kinda felt sorry for me.

James' father was a war veteran and was very proud of his status. He ran the VFW Post, hosted a lot of affairs for the community and like so many other ethnic fathers in the area, wanted his sons to follow his path into the military. Jimmy had four brothers. None of them went into the military. Neither did Jimmy. As I look back, I believe that they really didn't go because of their mother. She wouldn't let them. She would fix every problem they had. She'd do for her boys before she did for her husband. But I, being young and dumb, thought, "Shit! This is cool! These kids get anything they want."

We turned out to be a pretty good couple, Jimmy and me, and I started spending more and more time at his house. As time went on I really became a part of Jimmy's family. I began to think that maybe this is what a close family was really supposed to be. I'd be there anytime I wasn't at work or in school.

My parents were angry with even the little time I was at home, and finally kicked me out. After a couple days, Jimmy noticed that I hadn't been home all-night and offered to let me sleep at his house. So I started sneaking into his place at night when everyone was supposed to be asleep.

I don't quite know if James' mother heard me come in one night, or just knew I was over there when I wasn't supposed to be. But she told Jimmy that either I had to stop, or we had to get married.

By then I was out of school, and I'm pretty sure Jimmy had been kicked out too. I'd recently turned 18, and there was no way I could go back to living at my parents' house. And James actually cared about me. Though he had his faults, I can say that. He cared. How could I not love a guy who would give me a place to stay? So, we got married.

That was the summer of '68. I was with someone who actually cared about me, and I was free!

I was going to miss Clinton, because we began to drift apart after he was released from prison. But for the first time in my life, I was free. And I didn't look back.

*   *   *

It wasn't long after we got married that I began to see the truth about some of the things that "seemed" great at the Outlaw house. It turned out that the Outlaws had more money coming in than what they made in their store. As I mentioned, his parents' house always had a lot of people hangin' around. Card games were a weekend ritual. Early on I hadn't realized, but all those people were into a lot of shady activities. These people were number-runners, drug-dealers, fences. The Outlaw house was a meeting ground for all sorts of illegal dealing.

Now this didn't bother me as much as you might think. Most of the people were just trying to get by with a little hustle on the side. The average working stiff couldn't make it payday-to payday. You had to do somethin'. The Outlaws themselves were deep in the numbers game.

A lot of the black families in the Westbury area were actually being herded into New Castle, as if some high-up real estate tycoons were trying to make a slum or ghetto for the poor black folk. After maybe a decade all the good white folks had moved away. I said good white folks. A lot of their kids would come back on the weekends to hang out and score drugs. You were always tryin' to keep from falling into something worse.

Besides, when we were growing up our parents didn't care how we got money as long as we got money. I remember a few times later in life when Daddy actually bought drugs from me to share with his girlfriends. I thought being an Outlaw would suit me just fine.

7

MARRIED TO AN OUTLAW

*W*e were married young. There weren't a lot of alternatives, but we definitely weren't ready. I believe we were just playing grown-up. Neither of us had much of an idea of how to start a life of our own. We just stayed in James' parents' house. But it was never quite comfortable after that. And once we were together, James' parents were slow to just give him as much money. I guess that was their way of inspiring him to get a job or do something to earn our keep. But it really just frustrated him, which he didn't handle well.

James had always been into having fun. But those times took him beyond the occasional joint to developing a full on addiction to drugs. In that lifestyle you learned that the quickest way to ease your pain, or hide from it, came in a small plastic baggy. His addiction wasn't completely obvious until after I was pregnant with my second child. But soon it was clear that he'd started taking harder stuff. Being in that house made it easy to come by. And his condition made it even more clear that we needed money, however we could get it, immediately.

We each did little jobs here or there to earn some cash. But as I got closer to my due date, work became harder. This pregnancy was different from my first one. I felt sick more often. It might seem odd that I actually missed the adoption home. But I did. I thought about Miss Leena a lot during those days leading up to the birth of my second child. On February 4th, I gave birth to a second beautiful baby girl. We named her DeKova.

Everything seemed fine at first. But then I had doubts. I kept asking to make sure everything was ok, but the doctors and nurses assured me that everything was normal. Two days after the birth, the doctors and nurses wanted to do a blood transfusion on the baby. I had no idea of what was going on. Still in pain, and confused, they had me sign some papers. To this day I don't know what I signed. All I remember was that she was given a half transfusion of her blood. I know that because by the next morning the nurses were getting me to agree to sign more papers to give DeKova a full transfusion. The nurse told me they (the doctors) should have given DeKova a full transfusion the first time. She explained to me about the ABfactor that should have been flagged during my prenatal care. But it was not. Unknown to me during that time, the hospital had made a mistake.

The next time I laid eyes on my baby girl she was yellow and hooked up to a machine with wires coming from every which way out of her body. I just couldn't take it. What had happened?? What had gone so terribly wrong?!?

I was a wreck. Jimmy's parents, he and I all knew that it was pointless. But we were off to the hospital anyway. I've never cried as much my entire life as I did over those next two days. I cried and ached and cried some more. The pain was terrible. Another baby… gone. And this was worse. There wasn't any hope of finding her again like I still held for my Kiera. There was no hope. Just pain. Guilt. Anger. At myself, and everyone else. I began to accept what the voices in my head were saying: God was punishing me for giving up my first baby.

DeKova never made it home. She died in the hospital. I felt so inadequate. I was such a loser. I couldn't get anything in my life to go right. I would not go back to the hospital to claim her, nor could I go to her funeral. I just was not strong enough to face another lost baby. My in-laws handled all the arrangements. My parents? This was the beginning of our decade-long separation.

By now I don't remember if Jimmy offered, or I just

found it, or where the first drugs came from. But I took them gladly. I took everything I could get my hands on. I wanted anything that could stop the aching in my chest, and the voices.

The next period of time was a different kind of blur from the last. I didn't sit around sad and pitiful all the time. I just wasn't there. I was so trashed I didn't even make it to DeKova's gravesite. I'm sure someone in the house gave us some stuff on credit. I know I took a lot more than we could afford. And they knew what happened. Oddly enough, I've often found more compassion and honor among criminals than I did around other folks. At least, they thought enough to try to help me ease the pain. No one from my family even came to give me a hug.

As time passed I began to spend more time in the drug world. I did a few more jobs to earn some money. And some of the crew who knew what we'd been through gave me and Jimmy some work. I came to terms with the fact that my life was still pretty messed up. Although it was still better than the house I grew up in, it wasn't the best place to raise a child. I decided that the baby was better off in Heaven.

I did find out that the issue my baby died from – her AB factor – was something that could have been fixed. The hospital should have known about it earlier, even then.

As I gained distance from the passing it became increasingly important to me to find a way out of the Outlaw home. I began to see that I would never have a life if I stayed. An old dream resurfaced, and no-longer-distracted, I pursued it. I found out that State University of New York (S.U.N.Y.) Westbury campus was still taking applications for the fall semester, and there were scholarships available.

I didn't tell the Outlaws. I didn't tell Jimmy. Jimmy pretty much had his own stuff to worry about. He had caught a burglary case and was out on bail. His mother spent a lot of money on some high priced defense lawyer. Heck! Everybody knew Jimmy was going to prison. I didn't tell anybody. I just filled out the forms while I was out one day, and waited. When the letter arrived it shined. It looked like a life preserver thrown to a drowning person. I slept with the envelope in my hand that night. I was thinking clearly and was more excited than I'd been in a long time. Things were looking up.

COLLEGE GIRL

I started school in the fall of 1970. As a freshman
I had a dorm on campus and a roommate named Jill.
Jimmy had been a little sad to see me go, but he wasn't
angry or anything. I think by then he knew that he wasn't
really going anywhere. And if I had a shot, I should take
it. I never declared being married on my application just
to make sure everything would go as easy as possible. They
really didn't need to know about my old life anyway. That's
the way I saw it. I wasn't that person anymore. I was a
college girl now. I was starting out on a new life. And the
sky was the limit.

I went to class. I did my homework. I actually started

to make friends with a couple of the girls on campus. I didn't talk about my past. But we could talk about other stuff. They seemed nice enough, so we hung out a little.

I'd been at school two good months when Jimmy came to visit. It was genuinely nice to see him. I could tell right away that he'd been partying a lot lately. But he was still the first person other than Clinton to care about me. I showed him around the campus. We ate. We had a nice time. When Jimmy left that evening I felt good.

It wasn't until the next morning that I heard the news. Sally Jameson was in the hall talking to some other girl whose name I don't remember.

"Yeah, he'd broken out some of the windows. But I don't think he got away with anything. He was still in the admin building when the police got him."

I muttered under my breath, "Please don't let it be Jimmy. Please don't let it be Jimmy! Please..." I closed the door. I went to class sweating. I hadn't done anything, but I couldn't shake this terrible feeling in my gut. It gnawed at me all day. I felt the door open behind us in the middle of English class. I didn't have to look up to know that it wasn't some late student or campus tour. Nobody had gone to the bathroom.

The campus staff person walked to the front and told the professor that he needed to take me out. He then came and told me that someone in the admin office needed to see me. I think her name was Mrs. McKinney. We arrived in the office to find a police officer, two other girls who I'd seen around campus (maybe in math), and James T. Outlaw sitting handcuffed to a mahogany chair. I tried to control my reaction, but it was a waste of time. The girls had seen me with Jimmy the day before. They thought I would know who he was.

I can give Jimmy credit in that he wasn't the one who told them who I was. He was just the idiot that broke into my college admin office of all places. To this day I don't know what he expected to find there. Maybe he thought that all of the kids' tuitions were kept there... in cash. I don't know. But needless to say, I lost my scholarship. I had a day to get my stuff out, and I was being watched most of that time. I think Jimmy got off on a misdemeanor for that. I didn't stick around to find out.

So Jimmy was just getting deeper in trouble, with little cases, plus he still had the burglary case he was out on bail for. He and I tried to stay out of trouble but it was not in the stars. He actually fought his cases for about three years, and back then that was good for any criminal.

Somewhere during that time in our lives we did make another baby. October 9th, 1972, I give birth to Melinda. Shortly after Melinda was just starting to grow Jimmy had to go and do his time. He got something like 5 years in prison. Again, I was on my own.

When I left school I headed for the city. No more Outlaws. No more Barnes. Or so I thought. But city life would definitely be different.

Looking Back

I lost my chance to attend college in my early twenties because of someone else's mistake. I wasn't angry. I just kept it moving, as they say. This was an opportunity delayed, but not denied. For whatever reason, my life shifted and my educational pursuits would not come until later in life. The message here would be that God remains in control regardless of circumstances in your life. Even when it seems things have fallen apart, there will always be opportunities to redeem oneself, to start again, and perhaps to begin anew. No young person should feel badly because their circumstances may be unfavorable. There is always a second chance. Opportunities missed in your twenties can be pursued in your thirties, forties, fifties or even sixties. Remember a delay is not a denial.

9

THE FAST LANE

Life on the streets of New York was actually pretty good to me… for a while. I started living in the city and living the street life. Drugs, fast money, fast times, high life & low life. I traveled all over and met some of the best and the worst of people. I'm not looking for any justification of the path I chose to take. It is what it is. I've met some of the most extraordinary people on Earth. Some were really great at what they did. Any time a person can wake up without a dime to their name and by the end of the day end up with $2000 to $5000 or more, well, I must say, that's a hustler! Now on the other hand they must be prepared to wake up and not make a dime. You also need to accept the fact that sooner or later your ass will have to go to jail. It is what it is. One must know this going into the game.

"Street Life" is rarely a chosen occupation. Well, I have known some people for which that was their main goal. But for most of us, we just want a normal life – job, spouse, house, kids. We're headed toward those things and... somehow things just happen. Something might happen to you, in your mind or body where you can't work. Maybe something happens with your family where you just can't afford everything you need. Sometimes you just can't find a job. Unless you've got family that can and will help, you've got to find a way to get some money! That's just the world we live in.

Me, well I had the dream of getting married, the house with the white picket fence, three kids (2 boys 1 girl or 1 boy 2 girls), my husband the hero, the warrior. And the main thing was that I would never ever treat my kids the way my siblings and I were treated as children, or for that matter, as adults.

It just didn't turn out that way. And if you go enough days without food or a comfortable place to sleep, you'll entertain anything. You'll get desperate enough to do just about anything. I was constantly devising new ways to get by. I was good at the hustle. And it paid. It fed. It clothed. I'd do that before I'd let men use me. No more bullies. So I kept on.

Street life is funny because certain people got their

own way of living. Some people sell the drugs. Some people take them. Some people run the cons and some people constantly get conned, over and over again. Some people do the stick-ups and hold-ups. Others get stuck.

At the time I didn't know it, but I was well on my way to becoming one of the "socially disabled". I read that term somewhere a few decades ago, and realized they were talking about me. I was becoming a pretty ugly person.

*   *   *

I saw a little of Clinton while I was on the streets, but not much. We were both in the city most of the time. But we never did connect like before. It's not that we didn't get along anymore or fell out of touch. He just had his thing and I had mine.

Anyway, he got into some mess and ended up in prison. He left quite an impression on Nassau County Jail. See, at the jail they used to have this thing called "The Elevator Ride". The elevator ride was used to keep the inmates in line, show 'em who the bosses really were. The goon squad; big, badass cops would take an inmate on an elevator ride. When the elevator came down the inmate had to go to the infirmary.

"*He fell down,*" was all they ever had to say.

Yeah, right! More like their fists fell down on his face one too many times. But Clinton wrote me a letter once about his famed elevator trip.

"Goon squad comes to get me, right Sis. They walking me to the elevator, grinning the whole time cause they just know they 'bout to have some fun beating up on a nigga. We gets inside and the first thing they do is take the shackles off and I'm ready. You know me, right Sis? Yeah, them shackles came off and I was ready to rock. Anyway, another officer pushes the fifth floor button, talkin' 'bout, You ready, boy? Shit, ain't no thang, pig. And then we all got to fighting and shit. Elevator goes up, elevator comes down, we still tussling'. I walks out, grinning from ear to ear. Wasn't no infirmary for the inmate that day! See, the goon squad wasn't hip, ya dig, Sis. They ain't know nothing 'bout me being a fighta and all, so they learned the hard way."

At least, that's the way the story went as he told it. I'm sure he filled me in some more, added more details but I know Clinton. I've seen him fight. I know his story wasn't too far off the mark. And it wasn't long before I heard it from other people.

"Ay, you heard 'bout your brother? He's the man, whoopin' up on them pigs and shit. You Barnes' crazy as hell and know it too!"

Each thing either of us did added to our reputation. Clinton's fights. Mine. My hustles. His friends. On the street we had a name to uphold. We were known for being wild and crazy, fighting anyone like mad dogs. Even William and Kevin took up martial arts after Clinton. They got pretty good at it too. All of us Barnes were crazy fighters. It had to stem from our upbringing. We knew how to take

Kevin's high kick always looked painful.
Another dangerous Barnes brother.

a beating and we knew how to give one. But there was also a price to pay in the street life – you had to maintain a reputation no matter what that reputation was. As a drug dealer it was out of the question to let anyone ever get over on me. So it never happened. I never had a problem pulling a gun on someone and shooting. I never had a problem bustin' someone's head wide open, even if whatever they did didn't warrant an ass whoopin'. That was just the street life; there was no "live and let live" philosophy. It was dog eat dog out there.

But my little brother Clinton didn't see things the way they really were. He didn't see the reality of his situation.

William Jr. & our friend Eugene Johnson.

Yes, he could fight. He was a damned good fighter too. He made black belt in some martial arts discipline. Anyway, Clinton always fought, but he fought fair and honest which most other people did not. That's the part of his reality he never grasped. Not everyone plays fair. Not everyone knows how to take a beating, and leave it there – just respect the fact that you beat them fair and square. They come back. And not when you can see them. Not in the open. They don't look you in your face.

They found him at a Michael Jackson concert in 1979. They shot him in the back there on the concert hall floor. He died before he made it to the hospital.

We still don't know who it was, exactly. Probably never will. That's how some of these things go. My heart was used to hurting by the time I lost Clinton. I was angry, but I wasn't that surprised. If I could have found the bastards that shot him, I would have made them suffer every which way a man can. But as I said, I knew we never would. I just committed to pouring the love I had for Clinton into my daughter. She was my entire family now... or so I thought.

Looking Back

I play the street life.... Because there's no place I can go
Street life... It's the only life I know
Street life... And there's a thousand cards to play
Street life... Until you play your life away

You never let people see
Just who you wanna be
And every night you shine
Just like a superstar
The type of life that's played
A temptin' masquerade
You dress you walk you talk
You're who you think you are

Street life... You can run away from time
Street life... For a nickel, for a dime
Street life... But you better not get old
Street life... Or you're gonna feel the cold

There's always love for sale
A grown up fairy tale
Prince charming always smiles
Behind a silver spoon
And if you keep it young
Your song is always sung
Your love will pay your way beneath the silver moon

Street life, street life, street life, oh street life

– Randy Crawford

10

PATTI LABELLE'S BACKUP SINGERS

*W*hile living the fast life on the streets of New York I did also catch up with my older sister. She'd been hustling for quite some time. And once we met back up, we soon found that we made a good pair. Arlene was still just as crazy. So between the two of us, there wasn't anything we wouldn't do.

My sister Arlene (we called her Candi by then), her friend Betty and I were crossing the border from Canada to America with our loot. We'd driven up to Canada to make some money in Candi's brand new Buick. We were looking good, dressed to the nines, looking like the back up singers for Patti LaBelle.

Make no mistake, we had skills with good looks and money to flash. The hustle of the day was fur. We would go into a store and roll and pack a $70,000 sable fur coat into our clothes. You'd be amazed how tight and small sable rolls up. You could fit an entire coat in a pants leg if you wiggled just right... and wasn't wearing those tight ass jeans. We'd each get at least one while the others looked out. Then we'd head for the door, look the salesperson straight in the eye and tell them we'd be back. We'd walk right out with the coat between our legs.

This job worked pretty well for us and we had about four or five luxury fur coats each before we decided we were ready to leave the country. Back then no one needed a passport, and a fake ID worked just fine... most of the time.

As we drove back towards the States we were feeling good. We were talking and laughing, the music was loud and we had about half a million dollars worth of fur coats in our trunk. We were set. With half a million in loot, we were looking at an easy twenty grand each, if not more. And with Candi's high-end clientele we knew we'd get the loot off easily. Shit, everyone who was anyone in New York during the '60s and '70s wanted and wore furs. Didn't matter where they came from or how hot they were when they got them.

As I said, we were feeling good and really close to the border. We didn't notice that the car behind us had been following us for the past fifteen miles or so. We didn't notice that they'd sped up and began to tail us. But we did notice the blue lights flashing in the rear-view.

The Canadian police pulled us over and searched the car. Of course the first thing they noticed was the trunk full of fur coats. They started questioning us and all I could say was, "Canada is the coldest country I've ever been too. You need at least three or four coats."

The police didn't take too kindly to my jokes. Luckily they hadn't had any reports of stolen fur coats so our luggage didn't concern them. What did concern them was Candi's new Buick. Her license didn't match up to the registration and that gave them the power to take our car. And that's what they did.

So there we were, the three Patti LaBelle back up singers, walking back to the United States in the snow with our arms full of fur coats. We found a payphone by the side of the road and called to find the nearest Greyhound bus station. Then we got a cab to the station and we were on our way home with the loot.

We had to wait a long time after we bought our tickets. You would have thought buses to New York would be more frequent than that. We noticed a few cops walking around, surveying the station, but nothing caused any alarm. We also noticed all the crazies, winos and prostitutes walking around the station, mostly hanging out near the bathrooms. That's the way it always is with bus stations. The dirty, dingy bathroom stalls, its floor littered with needles and bottles, was where some of the nastiest things took place. At any given moment you could see people shooting up and johns getting their tricks. We'd seen the scene many times before, so no one needed the bathroom. We just headed to our bus, found some seats and waited for the bus driver to roll us out of town. Once we were on the bus we were so exhausted and so glad to be getting the hell out of Canada that we all drifted off to sleep.

During the ride Candi woke up to overhear the bus driver on the radio with the US authorities. He said he had three suspicious black women on the bus with at least three fur coats each. Sure enough there was an APB out for three black women last seen at that bus station.

Candi woke us up and told us what was going on. We knew we had to get the hell off that bus and fast. With no other option, we had the bus driver stop the bus right then and there. We couldn't wait for the scheduled stop. There was no way in hell we were going to quietly hand ourselves over to the police.

We threatened the bus driver with loss of limb to loss of life and he was so scared he just stopped the bus in the middle of nowhere and the three of us shuffled out, still with our loot in tow.

So again we were in the middle of nowhere, fur coats in our arms, trying to make our way back to New York City. We walked across a frozen lake in pitch-black darkness that night against a bitter cold. We were scared to death slipping and sliding on the ice, but eventually we saw a faint light coming from the window of what looked like a small store or perhaps a house. With no other option, we took our chances and continued the trek across the frozen lake towards the light.

It wasn't much of a store, but we were damn glad to find someone in it with the heat on. We burst through the door.

"Where's the nearest cab station?"

"You got anything warm to drink?"

"How fast can a cab get us to New York City?"

The man laughed as we fired questions at him. He thought we were joking. Apparently, we were a few miles outside of Albany and the fare would be around $200 plus the cost of gas. Money wasn't a problem, so we asked him to call a cab. Instead he offered to take us. It would be quicker and no questions asked, but he wanted the money up front. We weren't fools so we offered him half the money up front and half when we got there, otherwise we'd take our chances with another cabbie. He started closing up the store, the girls and I exchanged glances, figuring it should be fine we all piled into his car, with the loot and hot coffees to go.

*　　　*　　　*

At about half past two in the morning and we stopped to get gas. We'd only made it a little ways past Albany when we got pulled over by some cops looking for three black girls.

Damn.

The furs are in the trunk, thankfully. The cabbie who, by the way, is a white man is being questioned by the cops. Luckily, he's on our side telling the officers we were with him, but the cops aren't interested. They begin to question us and start rifling through our bags and the cab, all the while we're hoping they don't make it as far as the trunk.

"Where ya headed, girls?" asked the one of the officers with a menacing look.

None of us answered too readily. We didn't have a decent lie in the three of our heads combined. What the hell were we going to say? *We've hailed a cab in Albany at two in the morning to take us to New York City?* They put us in the back of the cruiser.

We sat in the back of the cruiser for at least 15 minutes before anything happened. Nervous, tired and cold with nothing but the loot on our mind, we finally heard something that would change our luck.

The radio from the police cruiser came alive blaring out the description of the three females they were looking for. All three of the females were dark-brown, scantily clad and slim with short hair. Candi could damn near pass for white. Betty was as big as a house. And none of us were scantily clad. It wasn't us.

We also picked up from the conversations that there was a detective that could identify the trio. So, we banged on the window to get one of the officer's attention and demanded that they get the detective to come I.D. us as the three suspects. After hearing that, the cab driver started asserting his rights as well, ranting and raving about his loss of fare.

Within a few minutes an un-marked car pulled up and the girls and I went rigid. Not one of us were moving. Our breath was hardly audible. First thing I saw was a shiny black boot and my heart sank. *Shit,* I thought, *it's the fucking Canadian cop we had a run-in with earlier.*

**My sister Arlene (Candi).
She always could work a fur.**

How had he gotten in contact with the US authorities so quickly? I mean, it was only a few hours ago that they'd taken the car and, why was the description of us so wrong?

The detective emerged from the dark-tinted vehicle and he wasn't happy. He had a personal vendetta. Apparently, the three black women they were looking for were a group of prostitutes who jumped him and cut up his face. I don't know if they used a blade, knife, their nails or what, but he was cut pretty bad. I didn't want to stare at his face for too long. As I said, he was mad as hell.

He took us out of the cruiser and did a once over.

He turned back to the other cops and said, "Do they look like a group of hoes?"

And just like that they left us. Well, one of the cops told us to get our asses out of his town. But he didn't do any more than that. We were on our way and happy as hell.

We stopped for gas maybe two more times. After that we were exiting off the George Washington Bridge. It was early in the morning, perhaps six or so, and the cabbie asked us where we would like to be dropped off.

"Any place that's close to good ole Harlem," I said. Didn't matter where, we were on our turf.

As we paid the driver, giving him a little extra for all the hassle, he actually said the trip was the most excitement and fun he'd had in a while.

"I'm going to make a formal complaint to the police department in Albany. The way they treated you ladies, and me in particular, was just atrocious."

We told him not to worry about it. It wasn't worth it.

"Just get home safe, man," I said.

As far as the loot was concerned, he never realized what it was... or he never let on. Candi slid him a sable for his wife or girlfriend.

Those coats went quick as I remember. But I held onto that particular loot a little longer than usual. It was just too sweet to give away.

Looking Back

Was it worth the risk to put our lives in danger to make money that we wasted on foolishness? I don't have anything to show for the years I spent with ill-gotten gains. At the end of the path of illegal dealings your money winds up in the hands of a lawyer. It's just not worth the time, effort and risk to your life. It would have been a wiser choice to spend my time and effort in college or just working to establish a stable family life for myself.

God protects fools and babies. I am one fool who survived the madness.

11

CYCLES

The problem with the fast life is just that. It's fast. The good times, the ones you hustle and work for, move so quick. The money comes fast. Like I said, I've woken up without a dime, and went to bed counting thousands I made that day. And that's not just me. A true hustler can build a small fortune in a day – depending on how good you are.

Now it's true, sometimes you might not make it home that night. Some amount of jail time is pretty much included in the package. Big cash. Big risk. Not necessarily a good deal. But you come to accept it. You come to see it as the best chance you've got.

The money comes fast. But it goes fast, too. There's often a high price to stuff on the streets. Keeping up an image. Partying. The occasional incarceration. The money leaves you just as quick as it comes.

People come fast too, and they'll drop you just as quick. You always have to be careful who you trust. And you always have to know how far you can trust anybody. Who knows what? Who can lay the blame on you for something you actually did, or worse, for something they did? And who might dime you out to cut their sentence?

The part that's hardest to see is how to actually leave it all behind, and really survive someplace legally. Street life catches you and doesn't like to let go. Some try to walk away from it. Some run. Many die before they make it, or make it out. And it's not like in some movie. There's no glory in it when they die. There's no cool theme music.

The good times fly by. The bad times however… they tend to last and last.

"Cocaine, cocaine… drove so many insane." I remember saying that to myself a lot. During that period of my life everything seemed like a constant hustle. I was constantly wheeling and dealing to keep a roof over our heads. It was exhausting. One minute I'm using heroin to overcome the daily pain of life, the next it's cocaine - jet fuel, and I'm speeding. Talking bout running on empty? It was insanity to the 5th degree.

I tried to play it straight a few times myself – times

when I just wanted a break. Had it worked, maybe I could have gotten out sooner. I looked into some small legit jobs. But I didn't find anything (available to someone with my record) that would pay enough to live on, let alone what I was used to making.

I tried welfare. But I guess I just didn't appear destitute or poor enough to get help. The girls in those offices reminded me of the sisters from the Nassau County Children's Shelter. Here were more women who were supposed to help mothers with young children. They seemed to be disgusted by the people they were supposed to help. To tell you the truth, I don't know why anyone would take a job "helping people" if you hate *people*. Dealing with those folk made me miss the street. At least criminals out there were more honest with theirs.

So... no government help. Well... whatever. Back to the hustle.

I got some work in the numbers game. During the late '60s and early '70s the Outlaws were in that deep. Jimmy Outlaw's father was a numbers runner and banker. And he made sure it was profitable.

They had a way of getting inside information at the racetrack. At the time there were pole climbers for day races and night races. These guys could actually look at the board, do the calculations and have the winning number before the race was over and before the newspaper had it printed. This was big business. Sometimes they would know which horse would win, and in others when the race was fixed. I would be given a few hundred dollars to bet on a fixed race and collect thousands on one bet. A couple of times I was given two grand and told where to go, which window to collect the winnings, who to give the money to, how much my cut was and most importantly to keep my mouth shut.

It was during that time that I met James Brown, and we had our fling. No, not James Brown the singer. This was James Brown the horse trainer. He actually trained some world classed winners in the racing world. James was highly respected by many thorough breed horse owners. He was licensed and everything. I met him through my sister Gayle. They got me a job at the track. He worked the racket with the horse trainers. Certain races were fixed. So he got the info as to which horses were going to pull back during the race so the agreed combination would pay off. That was big money with big people in charge of a lot of money. I guess you could call James my supervisor. He liked to keep an eye on me. I liked it, as it gave me more inside information on the races. And before long we were dating. By that time everyone saw Jimmy Outlaw and me as brother and sister more than husband and wife (including Jimmy and me). So I hooked up with James Brown. He wasn't a bad guy, I guess. In fact, he was actually pretty good to me... for a while. He got me an apartment in Queens away from Westbury. And I was blessed with my third child, Vidella

Brown Outlaw.

After a year or so we had to change up our hustle, because the runners at the track needed a new face. The authorities were always just a few steps behind us. But it was good money while it lasted.

I stayed with J.B. after that hustle ended... but not long after. Although he was good at what he did, he got to be too controlling. I stayed with him longer than I should have, thinking he was older and wiser. But not so. He was just older. He made good money, but he had a gorilla on his back (had a hell of a drug sniffing habit). I guess it was his promise to take me out of the drug life and away from the Outlaws that made me stay as long as I did. But I should have known that he wasn't going to go too far from the drugs, let alone help me and his child get on with a better life... not with a habit that big. *"Cocaine, cocaine..."*

I also came to realize that James was a rollin' stone. To this day we are still counting the children he fathered. James passed on some years ago. My daughter Vidella has had some contact with his family. But nobody knows everything. I'm sure he took some of his secrets and the knowledge of some of his children to the grave.

Just to mention how life is – it is believed that Vidella's mother-in-law, who works at a kidney clinic in Georgia, had James Brown as a patient. Small world.

Looking Back

Looking back, I wish I could have broken the vicious cycle of hustling earlier in my life. I wasted a lot of years. If this were the case I could have avoided taking my girls through the unnecessary drama and instability in their young lives. Although I clearly understood the risks and the consequences I faced I still made the choice to take those risks (over and over again) rather than to rely on a welfare system that denied us our dignity and left us with few options.

It was all about survival for me back then. I could not seem to secure a livable wage so I just did what I had to do and what I knew to do. My joy has been that my children have not had to repeat the mistakes that I have made and my hope is that my grandchildren, knowing my journey, will have better options and make wiser choices in life.

12

PRISON LIFE

I want to make it clear that I am not glamorizing the "Hustler" life style. I guess I just wasn't "true to the game" as they say, or maybe I knew I just wasn't cut out for the life. Fact stills remains once you get a record you don't get a get-out-of-jail-free card and go on with your merry life. These days they say, "it's hard out here on a pimp." Well it was even harder back then. Once Rockefeller got hold of your ass you were pretty much done. Even if you wanted out, there was little you could do legally and still manage to feed your kids. So many good people, smart guys I knew, got life, or died trying to get out of their bid. A lot of them just lost their minds. Some of us managed to survive. Most of us took more than one turn in the pen.

Although I did my share of dirt (I'm not claiming to be innocent here), my reputation grew far bigger than I ever was. I was just a small turd with a giant attitude. Whenever I went before any court, I was usually being judged for my family associations (from both sides) and being a repeat offender, more than any particular crime I got caught doing.

But everyone needs to know that living that life, sooner or later you're going to do some time or die. My later came, and I was sent up to Nassau County Jail for two years. (I was attending trials for several cases.)

Being incarcerated probably prevented my demise at an early age, even though I had a few close calls inside the walls of those penal institutions. "The word on the street," as they say, travels faster than the speed of light (and back then we didn't have cell phones). So the tales from the streets of my fighting and acting a damn fool preceded my arrival to the prison. On top of that, Nassau was the jail that Clinton escaped from. And later years the same jail that my brother William escaped from. He was transferred out long before I got there, but they remembered him. And therefore, once again I had a name and a reputation to live up to, or pay the price for. Clinton and I both were transferred to the Mattawan mental side for evaluation. It was mainly due to our disregard for authority and our propensity to fight at the blink of an eye.

The Nassau County Jail,
(the County Hotel)...

...no place you'd ever wanna be.

*   *   *

The fun started soon after I arrived. This first incident sticks in my mind because I was just so tired, so new and caught off guard. Though I'd spent some time in the local city jails, it was my first case doing real time in a federal pen. I was so new to it, that I still thought the guards were there to "guard" me. I thought their job was to keep the inmates from escaping; to keep people in line. I was wrong. I soon found out, that like the shelter, they thought we were there to entertain their asses with our misery.

Processing in takes a lot longer than the movies show. I arrived at one of New York's most treasured maximum-security institutions for females, and finally got to a cell after about 6-8 hours of intake.

Intake is a lot like the intake of cattle. They brand you (give you a number), check to see if you're young or old, if you're sick or well, see if you have any markings (tattoos), see if you're with child or not. Then you get the verbal lashing concerning the rules. Then you get something to eat, which you can't eat anyway, and you get sent to the showers.

Well I'm washing up and I notice this girl walking back and forth sort of looking at me in the shower. I think maybe she's supposed to clean the shower after I 'm done. So I get my stuff and start drying my hair as I exit the shower. This chick actually stops me to ask who's team I will play for?

"Team!? Play!? BITCH, get out my fucking way!" As I remember that incident, I just went to my cot, and tried to get to sleep as fast as I could. Not being in my right mind, I dosed off. I should have kept my ass on point, but I was really tired.

The next thing I realize, I'm being attacked by a group

of women. They're just kicking my ass. I was held down as I started getting kicked and hit with fists, feet and who knows what else. The girls tried to muffle their laughter, smirks and cussing so as not to attract the guards. But I sure was yelling. All I could do was grab hold of someone's arm and use that as a shield to ward off some of the blows. I did get in some good bites on someone's limbs, and I managed to dislocate a few fingers. Then, just like that, it was over. The big lights went on. The guards came in and I was in for a real surprise. That's when we had the show.

The guards felt like they couldn't see what was going on, so they allowed us to continue to fight. They just added rules to the scrap. Now it had to be one on one. Why didn't the guards shut it down??? And here I learned. We were there for their pleasure. So, I had to fight. Of course this big ass, black ass, mad ass woman stepped out as my opponent. She had the audacity to say that I was trying to pull her woman. [She actually just wanted to fight just to be fighting, and because I was a new person on the scene, but who was there to tell, and what good would it do?]

We fought, and I did hold my own even though I was considered the loser…(in that battle). But I wasn't going to forget it, and it wasn't over.

Here's the thing about underestimating a person you know nothing about. I just wanted time to recover from being tired and worn out; from being processed into this new institution. Maybe they didn't know about me. Or maybe they heard the stories and were trying to prove some point. But they obviously didn't know the type of person I really was, or they would have been far more careful from that day on. The guard too!

I got back to each and every one of them in time. Once or twice I had to have help to the infirmary. But you can believe that her ass was limping right along to the infirmary with me. As the weeks went along and I got a little more acquainted with my new residence I caught that big black ass woman just right! My mission was to use the mop wringer on her head, as it was my chore to mop some long ass hallway. As I said getting acquainted with one's surroundings is a key component to surviving. I knew her schedule for this particular month. I even knew the sound she made as she walked my hallway. She came around a corner and bam! It was on!

I hit her square in the chest with my mop wringer. I was a bit off my mark because that damn wringer was actually heavier then I thought. But I was pumping with adrenaline. I was in high gear and the chest hit was enough to sit that bitch down. From there I went to work, kicking, stomping and smashing her with the wringer. I vaguely remember not being able to handle the wringer the way I wanted. I'm not sure if she was trying to hold on to it or what. But after a couple seconds of resistance, I just grabbed the bucket with dirty water and splash, poured the water on her ass with a few good bangs on the head with the bucket.

Damn! That felt good.

It happened so fast her crew was just stunned. By the time the guards came around the corner my work was done. See back then the female prisons weren't as fortified as they are now. They just didn't expect the women to be so aggressive. Most of the women there just happened to be in a bad situation with a boyfriend or husband. Some others had such a large load of drugs on them that they had to take the wrap. Most had a somewhat normal family support system.

Then there were the women like me…I was just mad. Hell, I'd learned to fight from Sgt. Barnes and my brothers. Being in solitary confinement was something I looked forward to. So I was pretty much prepared. I just went from the prison I was raised in to the prison run by the government.

As my time went on, I did have other incidents and altercations to deal with. But that's life. What doesn't kill you makes you stronger.

Looking Back

I have always been in a fight. As far back as I can remember I had to fight. I've fought to escape. I've fought to be heard. I have fought for those I loved. I have fought for my girls. I have fought for my dignity. I have fought to stay alive. I have fought for a new life. I have fought to be loved.

It would be a long time before I learned when I really had to fight, when I had to stop fighting and when I could let someone else fight for me.

13

TURNING POINT

*D*uring those years I spent a lot of time in and out of prison. As much as I was capable and willing to defend myself inside, as much as everyone came to think twice before messing with me, I hated it. One year in prison drains years from your life. I tell stories of fighting and survival because that's what I've known. But today I would plead with anyone not to go that route. Heck, you just can't ever get that time back.

Prison hardens your soul. It magnifies the madness. The damage done physically and mentally is irreversible. You don't come out the same. To expect a person to come away from years of confinement and conform to the so-called social and economical standards of society is ridiculous. To expect that our prison system would teach anyone to be a nice and kind law-abiding citizen is absurd. It just doesn't work like that. And the fact that most ex-cons don't have options once they get out makes it even less effective. If we want a prison sentence to change an offender, there needs to be some way that they can live afterwards other than committing another offense. The closest thing to the "magic pill" would be to give them some money, or better yet, a job. But even if that were possible, what about the person? What gives someone the strength to be human after they've had to survive years of prison like an animal?

In between my prison stays I found periods of happiness with my girls. I even met another guy. Cliff was nice. Everyone else called him Booney, but I hated that nickname. I really enjoyed spending time with him. We had fun. All would be well until finances drove me back to the hustle. Cliff was nice, but he blew through his money too fast to support us. It was the "crack thang", or as he liked to call it, his "free basing baby." Whatever the fuck it was, it was Madness! I hated that shit. Many times I would just leave out from the spot and not return for days. He'd still be there when I returned with his car. Cliff is a good example of the phrase "a mind is a terrible thang to waste." This man was highly educated... hustled all his life, short con, long con. He never did any thing with the huge amounts of money he accumulated. Yeah! As usual I was drawn to man that was pretty much worse off then I was.

But, no matter what happened, I'm still glad I knew him. He gave me my next treasure. Cliff and I never got a lot of time together. I was back in the pen after we'd been dating for about six months. I was incarcerated again, and this time I was pregnant.

The DA's office had me held at Riker's Island while they tried to get me to turn state's evidence on somebody else. But it didn't matter. I was back in, and pregnant or not, I was back at war. In fact I fought so much that after a particularly bad scrap, I was put on bed rest and given a blood transfusion.

I spent a lot of time during that pregnancy thinking back over my life; my childhood, the street life, the daughter I'd lost and my Kiera, wherever she was. By this time I had two babies to take care of, and now a third on the way.

I knew that being absent from them must have put a lot of mess in their little lives. I thanked God that the girls had one grandmother that insisted on keeping them together. She kept them while I was locked up. Yeah, grandma (not my mother) kept them together. But she also made sure they each knew their peer level. She was caught up in that issue of dark brown vs. light brown and other foolishness.

They wrote to me. My beautiful little girls wrote to me. I still have some of those letters from my kids. It broke my heart then, and still breaks it now, to know the mess I put them through. They didn't make that bed and they shouldn't have had to lie in it.

"Oh My Lord! Will they ever forgive me?" I cried, lying in that hospital bed receiving a blood transfusion to save the lives of my baby and me. Here the prison nurse was trying to save my baby from the fruit of the lifestyle I'd chosen over and over and over again.

I tried to cling to the little sayings that were the foundation of my life. *Whatever doesn't kill you makes you stronger.* But it sounded hollow and pathetic in regards to my kids. How could I possibly put that on them? Long ago I had vowed not to let my own children grow up in a cold, loveless house like I did. It may be true, that whatever doesn't kill you makes you stronger. But it sure will leave some deep scars!!

I had to stop letting my choices and this system hurt my kids. There had to be a way out. There had to be a way to keep from repeating the cycle – to survive without breaking the law – to provide a loving home for my kids without the hustle. I vowed that day to find it.

*   *   *

I was transferred from Riker's Island back to Nassau County. After all that business of trying to get me to turn state's evidence in their big case, my attorney proved that I was not even in the same damn state as the crime they wanted me to testify about. So I was shipped back to

Westbury, stressed out, but free. I was just back in town, trying to decide whether to stay in Westbury or go back into the city when I went into labor. My youngest was born on February 11th, 1984. I decided to name her after her older sister. She was born Kiera Clinton Outlaw. And she was the beginning of my rise out of the street life.

Looking Back

There comes a time in life when we wake up. We awaken to new possibilities. We awaken out of our slumber and out of our hellish despair. I thank God that I woke up in time. I was graced to have a turning point. The birth of my youngest daughter Kiera was my turning point. This is when God's favor and kindness were shown to me in amazing ways. Things began to look up. Things began to come together for me. After all the hell I had been through, after all the reckless years...I was granted a turning point and a second chance.

PART III
Catching Butterflies

14

THE WAY BACK & TWO
BLESSINGS FROM THE OUTLAWS

*O*ne other memorable thing happened in jail before I was completely done with it. I met and married yet another James.

James McClain was a nice white man that I met through letters. He was serving in another part of the county jail. We were able to visually see and speak to each other when we went out to the yard. And through our correspondence we developed a friendship. We figured out that we got along pretty well. And as the weeks turned into months we started talking about being more then friends. Sometimes we were able to get a hug or kiss passing in the hallway (if the escorting guard was cool). And in time we wanted to be married. I wouldn't say we were madly in love or nothin' like that. But he wasn't a bad guy. Actually, he was a look alike for Lee Marvin; good looking, strong build, a real man's man. Plus it didn't hurt that he came from money. He'd made his mistakes, but there was also still a real life waiting for him when he got out. His father'd been some type of doctor or business tycoon. I don't remember exactly how he got his money, but I'm pretty sure his dad was dead. And James' mother was holding on to a pretty large chunk of money for him.

Now it also didn't hurt that when he asked me to marry him, I needed all the allies I could get to help fight my case. The State of Texas was trying to extradite me to Dallas to serve time out there. I was fighting that with everything I could think of. And being married to a man in New York with money seemed like it might help.

Well, James failed to mention to his aging mother that he had gone and gotten engaged to a black woman. I don't think she found out until the wedding day. And let's say, she didn't take it well.

Aren't people funny? She knew I was serving time. She may not have known what I was in for, but she knew I was inside. She could get past that, but couldn't handle the fact that I was a black woman.

She disowned him, and threatened to leave him with nothing. We did get married that day, but we never consummated it. James got out soon after that. He stopped by my mother-in-law's house, saw my kids and hung out with them for the day. He gave them some money, and I never heard from him again.

I don't blame him. I liked him, but truth be told, the money (and Texas) may have had something to do with me being ready and willing to get married. Funny thing was, he hated his mother. He thought I had money. I believe he was trying to get away from her. So we were both lookin' for a way out.

I laugh when I think of his mother, though. I know James. He liked the sistahs. He may have backed off that day to make sure that he got some of his daddy's money. But I'll bet it wasn't long before that old white woman had some black grandbabies runnin' around somewhere.

So I got another wedding, but not another husband. And my sisters got ammunition for jokes that they still make to this day.

"Don't bring anybody named James around our sister... she'll marry him."

"What's your name... James? Run Frieda, run!"

The day of the wedding was pretty surprising for one other reason. Jimmy Outlaw's father came to the ceremony. He was right up front with questions, wanting to know "what the hell is going on!" I knew that he was coming to make sure I actually got married and therefore wasn't entitled to anything of Jimmy's. But it was still nice to see him.

So now I was a McCain. Well, as we were never together, I never changed my name. And surprise of surprises, Texas didn't care one bit who I married. I was shipped out soon after to Ft. Worth, TX – Tarrant County Jail. After the customary and frustrating court proceedings, I was sentenced to 6½ to 10 years. I was then shipped off to Gatesville correctional facility TDCJ female unit.

It looked pretty bleak in the beginning. But my new attitude toward getting out and staying out actually helped. I managed to avoid people's attention. I kept fighting and problems to a minimum, and I was paroled in 2 years. I walked out of that damned building determined to never step foot in any prison again. I didn't want anything to do with any lawyers, any police, any judges, any criminals, nothing. From now on, my life, and the life of my girls, would not be governed by the rules of the places I'd been. Not my parents' house. Not the streets. Not the courts or jail.

Texas was offering me a new start, and I was taking it.

*　　*　　*

After all the threats and rigmarole they gave me about not turning back to crime, and not leaving the state (my new rules), I was given the address and directions to a halfway house on the south side of town. I found the place easily enough, and was soon standing outside a large white house with big brown doors. My mind immediately went back to the Nassau County children's shelter, the reform schools and prisons up north. My experiences with state-run communal living hadn't gone well. I wasn't expecting much more from this place.

The Way Back.

I went in, met with a resident overseer, and briefly met Mr. Everett George, one of the Board members. They called this place the Way Back House. Apparently, some big Northern Texas Methodist Church founded it not long before I got there. And the two or three other residents I spoke to my first few days didn't seem to think it was that bad.

One of the first things I noticed about the Way Back House, and my new life in Texas, was that it didn't feel like New York. Some days that was good. Some days that was bad. When you're hungry at two in the morning, it stunk. But being far away from the life I had also had its benefits. I'm sure it made it easier to go straight, even if those first few jobs were terrible. Sometimes I wonder if getting far enough away from New York, from Westbury, helped me get my life together. I guess some distance and scenery can be a really good thing.

It wasn't long before I had a job. It wasn't a livable wage, but it was a job. I started waitressing at a little mom and pop restaurant a few blocks away. That didn't last long. Neither did my position at Burger King. But someone was developing the land and building a strip mall across the street from the Way Back House, and it looked promising. I frequently stopped over there to ask what was going on. I had a feeling that a good position for me might open up over there. I found out that a brand new dry cleaner and laundry would be opening up soon.

I hung around the site for almost a month until I was able to meet the owner in person. I stated my case and got the job. It helped a lot that in my earlier days I'd worked at the Outlaws' dry cleaners back in New York. For a while James and I even ran it, until his drug problem got the better of his business sense.

But I knew how to do that, and do it well. So I started at the cleaners across the street, and during my time there worked a number of positions. At one point I was the silk presser, tagger, hothead operator. At other times I was the bagger and spot cleaner. I even did alterations. Over time I wore every hat needed when needed and implemented some new strategies that made for a more efficient operation.

I was getting established, and things had been looking up when I received a notice from the State of New York. I had been sued for child support. Now I wanted my kids with me, but not being able to feed them was what sent me back into the streets before. At that point, I would send what I could, but it was far from consistent. My pay was far from consistent.

I confided my situation to a friend over the phone and he sent me some money. Now I had a few hundred dollars in my pocket. It wasn't enough to bring my kids out to me and get us a place, but it was more than enough to get a flight back to New York, and get a hustle going.

Some would call it fate that on that particular day, the roll of cash popped out of my pocket while I was doing my own laundry back in the Way Back House. Others might call it coincidence that a resident overseer just happened to be there and see my undeclared, unauthorized, unexplainable cash hit the floor. But he saw it, and he told.

One of the well-understood rules of the Way Back House was that you could not have any undeclared money. You had to show your paycheck stubs so they knew all of your money had been acquired legally. And though I could (and tried to) argue that my friend sent me the cash out of the kindness of his heart, it still broke the rules. The resident overseer took me before Executive Director Albert Richard (which they pronounced Rï–shard).

I was ready to be yelled at and threatened, to hear some speech about my life going nowhere and possibly to be put back in

Al Richard.

jail. I didn't think that they could do that without proving that I had actually committed a crime, but I wasn't sure. I figured they could say whatever they wanted. As long as they didn't confiscate the money, I was out of there anyway. This wasn't what I wanted, but you get used to tough breaks after a while.

What I didn't expect was compassion. Mr. Richard did speak to me that day. But he spoke to me with respect, and with sincere compassion. He asked me what was going on, and I told him. I knew he was an intelligent man, but I hadn't had much experience with a compassionate man, or really any nice man for that matter that didn't want something from me in return. He convinced me not to leave, not to break my parole and invite another prison sentence. But not just that, he went to bat for me. Mr. Richard arranged for Mr. George to go to the court proceedings with me and help fight off the judgment. Then

Everett George.

the two of them helped me arrange to get my kids back and stay in Texas.

I have never, and will never, forget that. It helped me change. And it inspired me to think differently about peoples' motivation.

I got established. I made a friend – Joe F. He was another resident of the Way Back House. He got a job at a car dealership a little ways out from the House. And through him, I bought a car. It was a funny-looking little Ford Maverick. The color was Mexican rustic- orange. Today, it would be called a "hoopty". It *was* odd, but it was mine.

I can't explain how good it felt at that point in my life to have a legal job where I was earning a livable wage. Now "livable" may have been just below the welfare line. Plenty of nights I (and my girls) ate Ramen noodle soup for dinner. But the money was legal, and it was mine. And more than just the money, I was good at what I did, and respected, without it having to be about violence. I was beginning to build a life that I could bring my girls into and raise them in without shame. And I was finally establishing a life away from criminals… or so I thought.

ck

When God gets ready to move in your life, He will divinely connect you with special people. I call these people angels. Mr. George and Mr. Richard of the Way Back House of Dallas were two of my angels. I was disarmed by their compassion and fairness. They were not ordinary men. For me they represent genuine love and care. I had never met anyone that would go to bat for me and not ask anything in return. The world needs more angels like Mr. George and Mr. Richard.

15

CALIFORNIANS & AL RICHARD (PRONOUNCED RI-SHARD)

The day my girls arrived at the airport will always be with me. It was so full of different emotions that it was truly difficult to get through. I spent a long time that day reminding myself that I had to get my shit together. Things were getting better and I had to keep them getting better. I didn't want us to ever be separated again. They needed me and I needed them.

When they got off the plane my heart was full. I was caught up with how much I'd missed them and wanted to see them. I was pained to see how much they really weren't little girls anymore. Melinda was 15 years old. Vidella was 12. And my little Kiera was 4.

As they walked toward me I continued my mental declarations:

My girls' lives will be different from mine.
In our home we show affection.
They will know it doesn't cost you anything to encourage someone else — to encourage each other.
I will always tell them that they can be anything they want to be.
No one gets held back from being free or being successful.
I will always be honest with them.
They will always be able to talk to me.
Our house will be a safe place, where we can find peace.

I became a Texan that day. And things did change for the better.

That old Maverick may have been ugly... but it was mine!

The girls took some time to adjust. At first, Melinda didn't even want to get into my car. She howled in the airport parking lot.

"Mom, are you kidding me? That thing is ugly!"

She did eventually get into the car, but she wouldn't be happy in Texas for a while. She felt just sick without her boyfriend. For the first few days I got to hear how wonderful her boyfriend was. She actually went back to New York to live with her grandmother before long, largely so she could be with him. It hurt to see her leave, but I wasn't about to judge. And if the boy was all that she seemed to think he was, if he loved her as much as she believed he did, I would be happy to see her happy. But it didn't last. She came back to Texas after a few weeks, and we never heard about that boy again.

The girls also had to adjust to my new lifestyle. We had just gotten into the car one day when little Kiera saw a policeman.

She cried out, "Everybody get down, it's the Po Po!" All of us had crouched down on instinct before we remembered that we didn't need to hide. Now and then I both laugh and cry when I think back on it. I do have my regrets as to what I put my kids through. I've cried my tears over the early childhood that I was not able to give them. But I also have my pride and gratitude to God for what I, we, came out of and went on to.

As time went on, I finally stopped keeping an eye

out for police. My girls did too. We got a nice apartment. I got them in school. And we settled into a pleasantly normal life.

*   *   *

I had been working at the dry cleaners for about nine months when I had my next brush with the police. It was quite unsettling. But at least, they weren't after me.

Turned out this mild-mannered California man who'd built the dry cleaners was wanted by the Feds. He and his son had been indicted for money laundering and embezzlement as part of some mob bank out in LA. The Californian was the bank president (or vice-president). I couldn't believe my luck. Here I was just getting established in a legitimate life, and we were at risk of being closed for good and seized by the government. The Feds put locks on the doors and everything.

Luckily, the Californian had a partner who was cleared of any charges, and the dry cleaners stayed in business. But I guess the Californian was guilty. He put a gun in his mouth instead of going to jail. His son took it hard. All of us were hurt by it. He was a nice man. And I will always appreciate him giving me the job, knowing my background and all. But then, it turned out he was a far bigger crook than I ever was. But again, who am I to judge?

During that fiasco I took on a second job back at the

Way Back House. I became an ex-resident monitor (just like the one who saw my cash, ratted me out, and helped save me from going back to New York).

Yes, I needed the money. But really, I just never forgot the compassion and genuine help that

That's me at the Way Back House. And yes I was stylin' in that hat.

Mr. George and Mr. Richard showed me. Between the two of them, they'd helped me on many occasions. I knew what it felt like for people to know where you've been and know what you've done, and still treat you like a person when others won't.

Part of my job was to take the residents out to the movies on Friday nights. It's amazing how something as simple as taking someone to the movies can brighten their whole week, can show them some non-judgmental humanity. I know I enjoyed it. It gave me an opportunity to speak to some of them… to offer what knowledge or help I could.

*   *   *

I stayed at that cleaners and worked part time at the Way Back House for more than six years. And Mr. Richard and Mr. George continued to be an encouragement to me. At one point they actually helped me go to trucking school. It didn't take. To this day I still don't know how some of those guys back those rigs up as fast as they do... y'know without tearin' somethin' up. So, it didn't work out. I was back in Mr. Richard's office right after I failed the test laughing with him about it. I didn't let that stop me. Life was different now. As they'd shown me, it was full of possibilities.

It wasn't long after the trucking school that I found my current career in Ad Photography. Things became a bit more stable, and closer to the image of "normal life" that so many of us strive for. For me "normal life" meant not having the police in the rear view mirror all the time, not having to constantly worry.

My girls grew. I got married again. This marriage lasted longer than the other ones, but it still wasn't right. Dennis turned out to be a drinker... a violent drinker. Now, you know I wasn't going to let him just hit on me, so we had a few good tussles now and then. On more than one occasion they had to send two ambulances to pick us both up. Beva and Kiera hated him. And though I tried, we just couldn't get it together. He was broken with unresolved issues. I was broken with unresolved issues. We were two mismatched broken pieces. The only common denominator was the Way Back House. Us gettin' together was like tryin' to make a cake outta Vodka and Peanut Butter. So, we got divorced. But he had the better lawyer, so he got both cars. That was irritating, but I was just glad to be out of it. And my girls were glad. And we knew we were gonna be just fine.

And fine we've been over the last fifteen years or so. We've traveled and seen the world. I've owned homes, and cars, and everything you could ask for... or at least, everything I've ever really wanted (most important was peace, some control of my goings and comings, but most of all peace of mind... to be stress free as much as possible).

*   *   *

About seven years ago I found myself over at the Way Back House, sitting around and talking with Mr. Richard, when he asked me if I would be interested in speaking to some of the girls. I saw him pretty often. By that time Mr. Richard had been the Executive Director of the Way Back House for over 20 years, and had grown to be one of my dear friends. Sadly, I missed Mr. George's funeral. But I'm glad I visited with him at his residence while he lived at the senior facility. His passing on was definitely an awakening to my own mortality. Time waits for no one.

Over the years, Mr. Richard had come to see me as

something of a role model for residents. I was slow to agree to that. But when he asked me to speak to people, I couldn't say no. I would like to think I was able to impact a number of them in some positive way. I have gotten feedback and thank you calls from many. Not all of course. You win some. You lose some. People still make their own choices, and I'm not a fan of excuses. Not everybody listens. But I got the opportunity to see some of them do better for taking my advice. And that's a great feeling.

However, another of Mr. Richard's requests nearly got me fired. They were shooting a television commercial and wanted someone to speak on how beneficial the House had been in her life. As I had not informed my employer at the time of my criminal background, I refused. But after a promise that I would only be in silhouette and would be completely unrecognizable, I agreed.

Needless to say, I did the taping, and a woman on my job recognized me and approached me about it the day after the commercial first aired.

"That was you on that commercial wasn't it?"

"What are you talking about?" I said.

"I know it was you," the woman said.

"I don't know what you're talking about," I argued.

"The flip in your hair gave it away."

I stopped for a minute and thought about it. I hadn't taken the time to change my hairstyle before being video recorded in the spot...in "unrecognizable silhouette".

"Damn." There was nothing else to say.

That's how I met Nancy D. It turned out, the woman who spoke to me had some colorful stories herself. She just didn't take it to the next level. We talked and shared stories, and became good friends. Once again my thanks went to Mr. Richard. And the next time he asked me to talk to someone, I didn't even hesitate.

After a few years of this, Mr. Richard asked me to join the board of directors of the Way Back House. He said I brought a "much needed voice" to the board, and held the respect of the residents. So... I joined.

Over the past six years I've had the honor of fighting for those residents. I can honestly say I've done my best to encourage them that there is life after prison; a good life, an honest life, a life you can be proud of. I speak and share with anyone I come across who's dealing with issues; with a hustler's lifestyle or the temptation to start one. I tell 'em, "there is another way. The fast money is not worth it." These kids don't need drugs. They need a hug, some warmth, a little discipline and an honest voice telling them that they will be loved unconditionally. At times I still wonder what I would have become if I'd had those things.

On the board I fought to see people treated like people, instead of like 'ex-cons'. And I've seen the change in those people's lives when they were treated like men and women and given a second chance. I've helped residents get jobs. I've helped teach those residents how to keep the jobs they got.

I myself have found a sense of purpose beyond just survival and taking care of my kids. I've been blessed to see lives change. I've watched people find hope when they had none. I've seen people finally decide to stop drinking, partying and hustling to pursue something better.

My precious girls have grown up and become my best friends. The oldest daughter that I raised, Melinda, and her husband are raising their four children. She is a very successful underwriter in the real estate business. My middle daughter, Vidella, joined the military and got a degree in forensic psychology. She and her husband are raising their three sons. My youngest daughter graduated from the prestigious Southern Methodist University, a private four-year institution: the first in my immediate family. She is my last and as such was my final attempt to the keep the memory of my first-born alive.

As difficult as my life began, it's now found some peace. I have a good job doing work that I like, making a decent paycheck. I have peace in my home. I have a clean heart and a clear conscience. I can voice my opinion and not go along to get along.

Although I still don't understand much of why my life was so hard as a child, I'm the closest I've ever been to being truly happy and content.

Looking Back

    I am told that it is not about the destination, but it's really about the journey. My journey has been an amazing one. I've been in some dark, rough places in my life. The triumph is that I survived my life at all. As Oprah Winfrey says, "I have come full circle." Now I am blessed to say that I am no longer groping in dark places, but I am walking in God's glorious daylight. And my soul indeed looks back and wonders just how I made it over.

16

JUDGMENT

March 5th, 2008

"Hello?"

"Hello, is this Frei–?" Static and the rustling bags and mail in my hands were louder than anything else the woman said. I'd just gotten in from work and a short trip to the grocery store.

"What?" I responded. "I can't quite hear you. Could you hold on a minute?" I set the bags and mail down, and pulled the phone to my ear again. "Ok. Sorry about that. Now, who is this? And who are you looking for?"

"Well, my name is Keira Banks. I'm trying to find a woman named Freida Barnes."

Her name was similar to my youngest daughter Kiera's name, but the pronunciation was different. "And this is in reference to what?" I thought it was a bill collector trying to get information.

There was a short pause. "Uh, this is a confidential matter for Freida Barnes. My name is Keira Banks. I'm looking for my birth mother. I was born at Booth Memorial Hospital in Queens, New York on July the 27th, 1965…"

I dropped the phone.

I couldn't believe what I was hearing. I wanted to start screaming and yelling, but I didn't want to scare her either.

When you've dreamed about someone for more than forty years, searched for her, and then actually find yourself talking to her over the phone, you don't really know how to react. You don't know what to say. I had imagined this day for such a long time. I'd imagined how I would find my daughter; how we'd be reunited and she would meet her sisters.

I'd imagined her running into my arms a million times, like she was five years old, me swinging her around, both of us laughing and truly happy. But I'd also imagined her not wanting to meet me, being angry about the adoption, or worse, looking down on me as a mother, or looking down on me for the life I've led.

How would this turn out? Would she want to know me? She found me, which was a good sign. But if she got to know me, would she still be happy she found me? Could she accept me? Could she forgive me? Would she understand?

I picked the phone back up.

"I'm sorry," I said. "Dropped the phone. You said you were born at Booth, on July the 27th?"

"Yes."

"Well, then yes. My name is Freida Barnes. I had a daughter that day at Booth, and yes, she was taken from me and put up for adoption. I named her Kiera just before they took her."

There was another pause, which I needed as I tried to get myself together. My daughter continued. "I spoke with a lady named Pamela Slaton at an agency in Manhattan. She found you through a..." She went on to tell me how she tracked me down, that she lived in Virginia with her husband and my two new (to me) grandchildren. She told me that she and her husband were pastors of a church there. I so wanted to hear every detail of her life, but my own questions continued to distract me. I was just about to burst open as we ended our conversation. But before we got off the phone, we arranged to talk again soon.

I immediately called my middle daughter, Vidella. I told her and we celebrated together for a while. It wasn't until after I got off the phone with her and knew the information would be passed on that I settled down to really think about what was going to happen now.

For almost two to three days I was a mess. Nothing in my whole life had prepared me for that moment. And for all the strength I thought I had, for all the fights and storms in my life, this one knocked me to my knees.

My first had told me that she and her husband were pastors. Now growing up it was always in the back of my mind someplace that when I was really in trouble I should pray. But that was about the extent of my religious background. My family wasn't exactly church-goin' folk. Daddy hated preachers, and just about anything religious. We frequently heard about the "scam" those preachers were pullin' down at the church house.

"I don't understand why anybody'd want to go an' give all your hard earned money to some lyin'..." Daddy could go on for hours about it. And don't let a Jehovah's Witness come to the door.

Arlene told me that a neighbor took us to church once when I was two. Well however old I was, I sure don't remember it.

But I have had my share of those looks some women give you when they're clearly comin' from church, and you're clearly not. I didn't care. But I saw 'em. Most folks livin' the street life have an idea of what religious church people can be like, which is why they don't wander up in there. Deep down I knew that not all religious folks are like that. Mr. George had been pretty religious. But you don't find people like Mr. George very often. And I didn't know what kind of religious person my daughter would be.

Well, I hadn't lied to the three I'd raised. I wasn't gonna start now. I desperately wanted to reconnect with her, to learn about her life and meet my grandkids; to really become a part of her life, and make her a part of mine. But it would have to be based on honesty. I decided. We would be real with each other, no matter the consequences.

*   *   *

Vidella did her job. She told everyone from relatives to friends to even strangers about our news. I can honestly say that the joy of the reunion just went on from there. Nearly everyone we told celebrated with us. They were all shocked but happy and glad to know that I wasn't totally crazy. I'd always told my girls during the growing years that they had an older sister, and that they also had a sister in Heaven. I'd always told them that one day we would find their older sister. As it turned out, she found us.

I couldn't meet my first in person right away because we were both headed out of the country within days of her phone call. But we made arrangements to meet right after we got back. On April 8th, 2008, I flew to Virginia Beach, Virginia and laid eyes on my first child for the second time.

There are no words to describe the experience. She and her husband came to pick us up at the airport. I came off the plane, down the concourse, through security and I saw her. There was no mistaking her. I walked past those security guards and saw the spitting image of myself at her age. And she saw me. I stopped for a minute to take the moment in, and I walked over to her. She looked at me. And she greeted me. And she hugged me. I don't know how long the hug lasted, but I know how many years of waiting and hurting and wondering and crying it began to heal.

We looked at each other, and laughed, and cried and looked and laughed. We were both amazed at how similar in appearance we were. I stood and stared at this beautiful grown woman and saw the five-year-old I'd always imagined spinning in my arms. There's truly nothing like it.

My eldest Keira had spoken to Beva over the past weeks, and the two of them had hit it off. She joined us that first weekend. My youngest Kiera was still in Japan and unable to get back, and Melinda was unable to get away. But Keira, Beva and I had a wonderful time. Even my youngest Kiera's father came. Keira and her husband Steve took us back to their home. I cannot describe the pride and joy I felt as I walked through their house, seeing that she was happy, and successful, and whole.

Tears came to my eyes on several occasions as I saw the similarities in our habits, and style. The color schemes in our homes were the same. We both chew ice. I truly enjoyed meeting my new granddaughter, our third Keira, and my grandson Jordan. Meeting my daughter's family was more than I ever hoped for.

That evening we sat in her living room and we began to talk about what happened. As I'd decided, I told her everything. I told her the good. I told her the bad. I told her about Sergeant Barnes and her uncle Clinton. I told her about the day she was taken from me. I told her about prison.

And she received me. My daughter talked to me, and held my arm, and let me know that we were family. She told me about the pastor and his wife that adopted her when she was three. It turned out that my daughter's adoptive mother, Rose Taylor, loved the name Kiera as well. They decided to keep it, but change the spelling to Keira.

She told me about her time in New York. She told me about meeting Steven and getting married. She told me about my grandchildren.

She told me that she wasn't angry at me, that she was happy to have me back in her life. When that single great 40-year-old fear fell off of me, I knew that nothing would ever be that bad again. I had my daughter back, and the sky would never be that dark again.

The universe finally gave me permission to receive the gift taken away from me decades ago. I didn't have to show how tough I was, I didn't have to have A+ credit, I didn't even have to act white. For whatever reason, this was the time to be restored.

*   *   *

Since the other girls were not able to make it in April, we made arrangements to have a true family reunion that

July 4th. It was incredible seeing my children together – sharing this amazing reunion with my four girls.

The reunion turned out to be especially touching for my youngest daughter as she and her older sister share the same name. Kiera (the younger) is a very talented artist and has some profound thoughts concerning the reunion, so I won't speak for her. I'll just say she shares the joy!

Even with the passage of time and my two failed attempts to use those professional services to locate my daughter, we were together again. I'd always had both Kieras. I was raising the one there with me, and I kept the other close in my heart. And now the gifts keep coming… Keira (my oldest) named her daughter Keira, too. I actually have three Kieras, and I couldn't be a happier woman.

17

REFLECTIONS ON MOTHERHOOD & SERGEANT BARNES' LAST ACT OF REVENGE

I called my mother not long ago. Sergeant Barnes and I talk maybe once a month. She hasn't changed much over the years. She's slowed down as she's gotten up in age. She doesn't fight anymore (at least, not physically), but her mind is sharp. I guess the realities of age make the need to hit folk a lot less compelling. Then, she also doesn't have any more kids to raise. So maybe there just isn't anybody around to hit, or to blame when the Pepsi runs out.

I wish I could say that the same transformation that happened in my own story had happened in my mother's. But sadly, I can't. The traces of those old prejudices are still there. She still doesn't like Arlene. She's still mad at the world. She refused to meet my first-born. She has had little interaction with my kids at all.

It amazes me that my parents stayed together all those years considering how much they seemed to hate each other most of the time. But, I guess that's what happens when you refuse to deal with the difficult situations in your life.

Well, this particular day, I called my mother and had the second most surreal conversation I've ever had. As she spoke to me in casual conversation she chose to mention the latest news there at the house.

"Well, your father died."

"What?"

"He's dead."

"Aw, mom, I'm sorry. How'd it happen? Is Maxine there? Do you need me to come and help with– "

"No. It's done."

"What do you mean it's done?"

"He died last week. I had the men take care o' him on Saturday."

I was speechless for at least a minute.

"Mother. I don't get it. When's the funeral?"

"No funeral. I had him cremated."

I was speechless for two more minutes.

"Uh, when's the memorial... or service?"

"I don't know. Maybe we'll do somethin' sometime. I don't know when. We'll see."

The conversation that followed wasn't pleasant. And

that was the last I even heard about having a memorial.

As I've shown, my father wasn't the most loving or gentle man. He wasn't a saint. Lord knows he wasn't faithful to my mother. But he was... my father. I should have had a chance to say goodbye. It mattered. As intelligent as my mother is, she knew that.

Now I wasn't entirely sure if she didn't tell me out of her hatred for him or her hatred for me. I still don't know. I know it hurts not being able to say goodbye. It hurts knowing my mother did it on purpose.

But I also know, that no matter how, or how much people have hurt you, you don't have to let those wounds define who you are and what you do.

My memories of childhood are not filled with much laughter or smiles, just heartbreak and pain. The issues I've had with my parents were never really resolved the way I'd hoped. For me, the hardest part was just letting go. Nothing I did or could do has helped repair my relationship with my mother. She still has the same disapproval, disappointment and just pure hatred of not only me, but as time has exposed, my children and grandchildren. Just accepting and understanding that you can't make someone love you, especially when it's your own parent, is a heavy blow to take, and I've had to deal with it.

But no matter how hard the blows are, no matter where they come from, we have the opportunity to strive for something better. We have a chance to develop positive relationships that are sources of joy and strength. We have the chance to love and encourage each other, to treat people with humanity and inspire them to encourage someone else.

Looking back at my story I began to see that it was special. It needed to be shared, not only with my family but also with others. I know there are other women who have not yet been reunited with a child that they birthed at a tender age. There are young adults wondering about their birth parents. And I know how the primary concerns with day-to-day life (and our fears of painful outcomes) tend to push dealing with such thoughts to the bottom of our to do lists. But this is the thing: Life is so short that by the time you look up it's just about over. So don't waste time. Take the chance.

Fill that void. Ask for help. Give help to others. Put it out to the universe. Mothers, reclaim that gift. I'm not suggesting that you try to take your children away from good homes if they've been adopted. But look for them. Find them. Make sure that wherever they are, they know you love them, even if you can't keep them with you right now.

Children wanting to find pieces to the puzzle, look for your birth mother. All that we seek we shall find. What we find may not necessarily be what we want... but the attempt is worth the risk.

But do whatever you have to do to restore those relationships. Value the people in your life, and give the ones you love your best. Learn, as I did, that 'you don't have to be your mother.'

*   *   *

Over the years, the decades, I've tried very hard to heal and release a lot of mess. Now I know I wasn't privy to the best psychologist, or even the pleasure of landscapes that could help a person feel good. I used to say, "I've always been a soldier in the war on poverty." But I knew I needed to get something done to fix what was going on inside of me.

I have always been a person to speak with God or to God at any given time. As by now I'm sure you know I was never the religious type. I'm not big on tradition. I don't know the protocol of the church. I couldn't tell you much about what the bible says. But I do know I can pray anytime anywhere. I do know to ask for divine help. Man has never failed to fail me. Hell, I've even failed myself. So being in such bad shape, I knew I couldn't make it without God's help. Looking back I clearly see many places where that help arrived. I see God's divine intervention that brought my girls and me through our storms.

I think back to days like the day the cut detective told the other policemen to let us go, and the day the money popped out of my pocket in front of the resident overseer at the Way Back House, and the day Mr. Richard asked me to speak to some of the lady residents. And I thank God.

I found out that 90% of the time, the children of women who've spent time in prison go on to do the same thing. I thank God for helping me guide and raise my girls not to follow my path. They beat the odds. I look at the parents that adopted Keira, and I thank God for the decent home she grew up in.

During one of my conversations with my oldest we discovered that she was at the same Michael Jackson concert in '79 where Clinton was shot. I like to think that Clinton saw her in the crowd sometime before they got him; that he caught a glimpse of this 14-year-old girl who was the spitting image of me at that age, and just knew that he was looking at his neice.

As I've come to learn, the God of the universe has answered my prayers and allowed my life to come full circle. As I enter the winter of my life the journey will continue with not one Keira, but three. I now have nine grandchildren instead of seven. And boy do we have stories and adventures to share.

This still amazes me!

As I sat on a couch in my daughter's den, my first Keira handed me a book. I looked it over and smiled with even greater pride and joy to see that it was the first book she'd written. It's called *The Matriarchal Dimension*. As Keira is a teacher and pastor and very bright, it didn't surprise me that she'd written a book. But what amazed me, and amazes me to this day, is that it is a book about the importance of a mother. This book she wrote just before she met me and learned my story, teaches how mothers throughout history have shaped not just children, or their homes, but the world. It's a book about a mother's impact. It calls women to become the mothers that they should and can be; the mothers of movements and businesses and systems. It says how important mothers are, and how they've been undervalued. It says what happens when a mother is not in place, or a mother's guidance and touch are not felt. It says what can happen when they are.

I thank God for that. The daughter I lost and regained is actually helping me grow closer to God and learn more about Him. I thank God for that.

We all have a story. Most are filled with some good stuff, some bad stuff, and how we chose to respond. As a person who has truly made the wrong responses on many occasions, and still seen my life turn around, I can say, no matter what you've done, there is hope for tomorrow. There is always some opportunity to make yourself a little better, and make your life a little better. And if you're willing to try, there is help out there for you.

The metamorphic process in my life is still at work… some days are as the saying goes, better than others. But I do thank the Lord every day, several times a day, cause I

My three Keiras: Keira - my first-born, Kiera - my youngest daughter, and Keira Iman - my precious new granddaughter. And like a good sister and aunt, Vidella watches over them.

remember my life in the past. I know that I'm blessed to have my children – my four strong women of substance. I realize that God was with me and my first-born daughter, for her to seek me and her biological sisters out. That was a day I will never let forget.

My daughters rejoice with me, and have expressed their own thoughts about what God has done:

Kiera, my youngest, said this:

"I was the lucky last, born in 1984. By the late 80s Mommy was settling down and finally on track to normalcy. While my older sisters, Hymie and Beva, have their fair share of stories about growing up with and without Mommy, I don't really have that many. I was too young to

really understand or remember anything. The memories I do have were always pushed to the back of my mind. I never dwell on the past because my mother has always encouraged me to look towards the future. If it weren't for my mother, I wouldn't be where I am today or who I am today.

We all see life through a kaleidoscope, the cascading images twirl in and out of our perspective and sometimes we don't see things as clearly as we should. Sometimes our memory plays tricks on us, provoking us to mix and match the pieces of our lives as if it were one sequence, as if these things happened in order, as if these things happened at all. I'm not saying Mommy is a saint. I am aware that her past is dark and twisted, but any path always has a light at the end that you either follow or ignore. I am grateful that she recognized that light as herself and fought through.

Vidella, Keira and I!

Vidella wrote:

"Even though my mother was not physically, emotionally, and financially supportive everyday of my life as a child, her life's journey has given me more valuable things. By that I mean the reason for her absence was a life lesson in itself. My mother's mistakes allowed me the opportunity to be a better mother, wife, and person overall. I think that it also made our relationship strong. I am extremely proud of my mother for overcoming her addiction to drugs, making horrible decisions that have landed her in prison and having the strength to realize that she does not have to settle for the bottom of the barrel in a companion. I love her for being honest with me, which made her a great mom in my eyes.

When I first laid eyes on Keira Banks, my initial thought was 'WOW, about time.' She looks more like my mother than the rest of us. We always knew that we had an older sister and it was just a matter of time before my mother found her or she found my mother. I am very thankful to the Taylor's for opening their hearts and loving her. I am proud of her not only for her accomplishments but also for developing into a strong, LAW-ABIDING citizen. My husband and I always debate on the issue of "heredity vs environment" [whether our parentage or childhood surroundings are more powerful in shaping who we become]. He says it's the genes. I say it's the environment. Well, this is another example of how I am right (lol). Life IS what you make it and we are all just fine."

My four girls.
Left to right: Keira, Melinda, Kiera (my youngest) and Vidella (in front).

Melinda had this to say:

"No matter what my mother was going through, she always made sure my sisters and I were ok. Through her honesty with us, never hiding anything from us about the lifestyle she was living, she has made me a better mother to my children, a better wife to my husband and a better person overall. We've always known that we had a sister in the world. Reuniting with her is the

*missing piece my mother needed to complete her transformation
into the beautiful rose she is today."*

My first-born, Keira Banks, said this:

*"My reunion with Freida was an incredible time of
healing, restoration and celebration for both of us. Our initial
talks and visits were like two old friends catching up after many
years. It was just delightfully warm and comforting all at the
same time. Since that time I have found out that Freida had
some initial concerns since I serve as a Christian pastor married
to a bishop. In her heart she wondered if I would judge her
for her past or if I would be able to accept the circumstances
of her life.*

Firstly, I made it a point to assure her that I could not be more proud of her and the challenges she has had to overcome in her life. Second, I shared with her that each and every person is on the planet to be healed. Despite our grandiose beliefs about ourselves, humans are imperfect creatures. I let her know that all humans are hopelessly flawed and the bible does not hide that fact. God has always chosen flawed and failed individuals to do His work and to accomplish great things in their lifetimes. Unfortunately religion has promoted the misconception that some individuals are blameless and that humans have the ability to live without blemish. This too is an erroneous notion. We are victims of our own indoctrination. Our misconceptions about human perfection lead us to believe that God is angry and ready to punish those who make mistakes. Somehow Christians have been duped into thinking that they are superior to those who fail to meet this standard of perfection. Therefore, we judge when we should have compassion, we condemn, when we should restore, we punish when we should show kindness and understanding.

The fact is that God is the only one who has the authority to judge anyone. Humans

judging and condemning other humans is laughable since every human is flawed, broken or dysfunctional in one area or another. Furthermore, no judge would try a case without having all the facts. Humans are not qualified to judge because only God could possess all of the facts of each and every case. Often religious people have an ego need to feel superior to others and so they unfairly penalize others. Jesus said, "Judge not, that ye be not judged. For with what judgment ye judge, ye shall be judged: and with what measure ye mete, it shall be measured to you again." (Matthew 7:1,2) I have learned not to judge but to extend love and mercy.

The fact is that no one is better than anyone else. We are deluded into thinking that people who get themselves into trouble are of less importance to God and to what He desires to do in the world. We are quick to demonize the failures of others when we should seek to humanize people in difficult circumstances knowing that dysfunction is a part of the human *experience. I know for sure that people who make choices that lead them down difficult paths are people in spiritual crisis. These are people who are in a great search for healing and wholeness. My mother's entire life has been a search for healing, wholeness, affirmation and love. People in spiritual crisis are in need of our love and compassion not our scorn and rejection. People betray and abandon each other…God never does…even when we are dead wrong. That's why His love and grace are amazing and beyond anything we can comprehend in the flesh. To be a Christ-follower means that you possess the capacity to* become *the love that others so desperately need. Without*

Keira Taylor-Banks and Freida Barnes at our mother and daughter reunion.

this love, Christ is misrepresented. I rejoice knowing that my mother's life is a miracle. The miracle is not that her journey has been without test and trial, but the miracle is discovered at the end of the day when she can look back and see all that she has overcome.

"Now abide faith, hope, and love, these three; but the greatest of these is love." - I Corinthians 13:13

*   *   *

Sometimes I think back on my brother's childhood image of me – chasing butterflies through the fields. In retrospect, I may have never been able to catch those butterflies. I guess even as a child I just wanted to capture the goodness, find something pretty in life. It took a while. The hardness of life made beauty elusive. But I now catch those beautiful butterflies, just like I finally caught on to the goodness of life. I now tell others not to give up the chase. The methods may be different than you think. But with a little patience, a little love, a little help from above, the beauty will come to you.

– *About the Author* –

$\mathcal{A}$long with her job as a photo stylist, Freida serves on the board of the Way Back House. She also volunteers with the House residents heading up the "challenge group", a regular meeting for male and female offenders to help them successfully reintegrate into the general public. She is currently working with Way Back House Executive Director Al Richard to open a service center for ex-offenders to assist them in the re-entry process from prison back into society. Freida lives in Irving, TX.

"My goal as a board member and volunteer for the Way Back House is to carry on the tradition and the spirit of Everett George. If I can muster up his energy and enthusiasm to help any resident get back on track, then my true assignment is being addressed. We all deserve to have someone care enough to give a damn about us, and help us get where we need to be. We all deserve a second chance."

– Freida Barnes

— *In Memoriam* —

EVERETT GEORGE

Your grace and ministry live on.

Made in the USA
Charleston, SC
23 June 2013